THE MYSTERY OF DEATH
AND THE POST-MORTEM COURSE OF THE SOUL

This book has been edited by:
Ilias Lampros Katsiampas
Vassiliki L. Katsiampas
Sophia A. Skoumis – Katsiampas
Anatoli Fitopoulou

Cover: Mediterra Books
Production supervisor: Platon Malliagkas – mediterrabooks.com

ILIAS L. KATSIAMPAS
OMAKOIO OF TRIKALA
METAPHYSICAL STUDIES IN YOGA AND SHIATSU
KEFALLINIAS 21, 42131, TRIKALA, GREECE
Website: http://www.omakoio.gr https://omakoio.blogspot.com
E-mails: omakoio@omakoio.gr or omakoio@gmail.com

©2016 ILIAS L. KATSIAMPAS
All Rights Reserved. No part of this publication may be produced in any form or by any means, including scanning, photocopying, or otherwise without prior written permission of the copyright holder.

First English Edition 2016

ISBN 978-960-85735-7-4
Trikala, Greece

ILIAS L. KATSIAMPAS
ESOTERICISM FOR ALL

THE MYSTERY OF DEATH
AND THE POST-MORTEM COURSE OF THE SOUL

Revelational descriptions and full explanations about the post-mortem course of the soul, according to the testimonies of the Great Mystics of Humanity and especially of Nikolaos Margioris, the contemporary Greek Mystic, writer of 189 philosophical, spiritual and practical works:
The structure of our world, Body-Mind-Intellect-Soul-Spirit, the 7 phases of death, the second death, natural and pathogenic transmigratory states, cremation or burial, astral punishment and respite, the Karmic Committee, the continuation of the evolution of the soul.

OMAKOIO OF TRIKALA, GREECE
FIRST ENGLISH EDITION, 2016

CONTENTS

DEDICATION	9
DISCLAIMER	11
WARM THANKS AND CONGRATULATIONS	14
WHAT ESOTERICISM IS	17
ESOTERICISM FOR ALL	18
THE MEANING OF THE WORD OMAKOIO	19
WHAT A MYSTIC IS. WHAT A MYSTICIST IS. WHAT AN OCCULTIST-OCCULTOLOGIST IS.	21
ACTIVITIES OF THE OMAKOIOS OF TRIKALA AND THESSALONIKI ESOTERIC PHILOSOPHY, YOGA AND SHIATSU	30
NIKOLAOS A. MARGIORIS, THE SPIRITUAL MASTER AND CONTEMPORARY GREEK MYSTIC	33
INTRODUCTION	37
CLARIFICATION	42
PREFACE	44
THE BASIC STRUCTURE OF OUR WORLD ACCORDING TO THE EXPERIENTIAL METAPHYSICAL VIEW	55
SPIRIT, SOUL, INTELLECT, MIND, BODY	64
THE MYSTERY OF DEATH AND THE POST-MORTEM COURSE OF THE SOUL	73

THE CAUSES OF DEATH	140
WHAT IS DEATH?	146
DEATH AS BENEFACTOR	155
THE PICTURE ON THE COVER OF THE BOOK *LIFE AFTER DEATH* BY NIKOLAOS MARGIORIS	160
EPILOGUE	165
EPILOGUE OF THE ENTIRE WORK	169
CURRICULUM VITAE OF ILIAS KATSIAMPAS	172
SHORT BIOGRAPHICAL NOTE ON PYTHAGORAS AND ON NIKOLAOS MARGIORIS OR "THE OMAKOIO OF PYTHAGORAS AND THE WORK OF NIKOLAOS MARGIORIS"	175
THE WORK OF NIKOLAOS MARGIORIS AND THE OMAKOIOS	183
SUMMARY OF THE WORK	198
BOOK REVIEW OF THE MYSTERY OF DEATH AND THE POST-MORTEM PATH OF THE SOUL	200
SCHOOLS IN OPERATION AT THE OMAKOIOS OF ATHENS, LAMIA AND TRIKALA	202
IN THE OMAKOIO OF TRIKALA THE FOLLOWING DEPARTMENTS ARE IN OPERATION:	205
BIBLIOGRAPHY OF THE BOOK	210

BIBLIOGRAPHY OF THE WRITER   212

I) PUBLISHED BOOKS
BY NIKOLAOS A. MARGIORIS
(copyrights belong to his heirs)   212

II) ESSAYS BY NIKOLAOS. A. MARGIORIS   217

III) OMAKOIO JOURNAL
BY NIKOLAOS A. MARGIORIS (49 issues)   219

IV) ESOTERIC KEY
BY NIKOLAOS A. MARGIORIS   220

BOOKS BY ILIAS L. KATSIAMPAS
(N. MARGIORIS' STUDENT)
OMAKOIOS OF TRIKALA
AND OF THESSALONIKI, GREECE
(AND YOGA ACADEMY
OF NIKOLAOS MARGIORIS – OMAKOIO)   222

GREEK WRITERS WHO USED EXCERPTS
FROM THE WORKS OF THE AUTHOR
AND THE MODERN METAPHYSICAL MASTER
NIKOLAOS A. MARGIORIS
(AND CITED IT IN THEIR BIBLIOGRAPHY)
(Search and classification by his student
Ilias L. Katsiampas)   226

PRESENTATIONS IN YOUTUBE
AND ON FACEBOOK OF
WRITINGS OF MODERN GREEK MYSTIC
NIKOLAOS A. MARGIORIS (1913-1993)
AND OF 14 BOOKS OF HIS STUDENT
ILIAS KATSIAMPAS -With English Subtitles-   238

PAGES ON THE FACEBOOK: 241

DEDICATION

The present work is dedicated to all incarnated souls of our world as one MORE ray of light to illuminate their way in the labyrinths of the material life that complicate, disorientate and distort their course. We hope that this book will constitute one more Ariadne's Clew for the gradual rediscovery of the road of return of every soul to the One Knowledge and the Light of the True Spiritual Life. I wholeheartedly wish that for all of us.

The Writer
Ilias Katsiampas

DISCLAIMER

Ilias Katsiampas, the writer of this book, has tried to convey the vast body of fundamental and important knowledge he gained from the perennial personal relationship and the close teachings he had with his spiritual Master, Nikolaos Margioris, in order to correctly advise anyone interested in the profundity of the **Esoteric-Metaphysical Philosophy** derived from a very few of our truly experiential fellowmen (Mystics), and particularly, in the phenomenon of the post-mortem life and the transmigratory course of the soul of every man, as well as in the catalytic role the relationship between the Master and the Student plays throughout the course of ascent and spiritual evolution.

The firm belief of the writer is that along with any specialized information and analysis that the present book provides, it also helps man to comprehend and perceive the supreme value one's esoteric cultivation has for oneself and for the community, and it encourages him to commune with and to reconsider the moral values and testimonies of the **Great Spirits of Humanity** on earth so that each of us may more responsibly assume our personal duties as individual, social and spiritual beings before ourselves and before the animate and inanimate Creation-God.

Every teaching, in particular that of a Metaphysical nature, presupposes a close relationship and regular contact between the Master (Guru) and the Student (Cela) on a daily basis (See our first book with the title *From the Master's Mouth to the Student's Ear* available on Amazon). The title of this first book was inspired by the second principle of **Niyama** of **Raja Yoga** that in modern times is interpreted-presented as **"the study of books dealing with the spirituality-liberation of man"**, while in the past, when there were no books on this subject, there was the everlasting personal teaching relationship (*From the Master's Mouth to the Student's Ear*) so that initiation is continually evolutionary, reliable, qualitative, substantial, true, vibrant and more effective. Any other relationship, such as the present one through the book, is of a purely and solely informative nature with the potential to develop the moral-spiritual evolution-perfection of every person, as long as this person wants it and follows it of their own free will within the framework of a close didactic training course and disciplined application in daily life as well. Everything else is wrong and unworthy.

The writer has made every effort to render the

subjects he is addressing comprehensible for the reader and he is in no way responsible for possible errors, inaccuracies, omissions or contradictions that may be encountered in the present book due to the free translation of the book from Greek into English, or that may be considered as such by the reader as a result of his insufficient or non-existent esoteric education.

Nor does the writer assume any responsibility for whatever misunderstanding, misinterpretation or side effect, since the book does not comprise a personal life coach but a descriptive-informative means of information and a provision of knowledge by the writer, which everyone is free to consider, question, judge, accept or reject.

We all wholeheartedly hope you find this study-course in the **Esoteric Experiential Knowledge of the Mystics** interesting, pleasant and useful.

Greece, Trikala, 1-12-2014
Ilias L. Katsiampas

WARM THANKS AND CONGRATULATIONS

I wish to wholeheartedly thank my sister **Vana**, student of Master N. Margioris and co-traveller – direct associate of the works of the **Omakoios of Trikala** and **Thessaloniki** and now **vice-president** of the Association **Academy of Yoga Nikolaos Margioris – Omakoio (AMOY – Academy Margioris Omakoio Yoga)**, and my wife **Sofia Skoumi**, member of the same Association and dedicated assistant of my work.

I would also like to thank a fellow student in the teachings of Master N. Margioris and a spiritual companion, **Niki Foufa**, responsible for the **Omakoio of Loutraki** and **Secretary General** of the Board of Directors of the Association AMOY, for her unreserved support in every initiative that I take in the multifaceted promotion of the Master's work and of the Omakoio. The contribution of all the people mentioned above for every need of the work we have undertaken was and remains important, direct and catalytic.

The same holds true for former students of the Master, such as **Alekos Papavassiliou (deceased), Kostas Mantzikos and Anna Giavashi,** who are concurrently developing their own activities within the framework of the Master's work, as well as for other fellow students, all of whom constitute active members of the Association AMOY (Yoga Academy of Nikolaos Margioris-Omakoio), which I had the honour of establishing with their cooperation and the support of my students.

I owe equally warm and whole-hearted thanks to the beloved soul of my spiritual mother, **Labrini Kaghialari- Polizoi**, student - close associate of the Master, for her continuous support throughout all those years of my apprenticeship beside the Master, as well as later, after the transmigration of Master N. Margioris, as well as of many other of my fellow students.

Also, I would like to warmly congratulate all my newer students from the **Association AMOY** and the older ones from the **Omakoio of Trikala** and **Thessaloniki**, each of whom, according to their strengths and skills, individually strives for the best in relation with the Master's work but also for their own further evolution on their esoteric course.

Among them Christos, Maria, Stratos, Voula, Thalia, Vivian, Sofia, Stergios and Cornelia, Irene, Panagiota, Giannis and Efi, George, Giannis, Christos, Athina, Lefteris, Sakis and Maya, George, Argiris, Vasso, Eleni,

Georgia, Mary, Christos, Giannis, Styliani, Kostas and many others.

I owe particular thanks to **Christos Manassidis** and **Athina Kirtsou** for their special contribution to the work of the Master through the Omakoio of Trikala-Thessaloniki; to my student, **Vivian Doufa**, for volunteering to translate various works into the English language and for transcribing my speeches; to **Irene Mylona** for volunteering to transcribe my speeches; and to my old fellow students **Niki Foufa** for translations into the French language, and **Kostas Mantzikos** for translations into the Spanish language.

Also, I'd like to congratulate my fellow students **Smaro Kosmaoglou** (Omakoio of Athens), **Dimitris** and **Koula Tsapara** (Omakoio of Lamia and now Pythagorio Omakoio) on their work, who, like I, undertook to fulfil the work of the Master directly by him while he was still alive and are making their own separate steps in the progress and evolution of his work.

Still, I take delight in and congratulate all those fellow students of mine, older and younger, who, after the Master's transmigration, undertook didactic initiative in one or more fields of his pedagogical work and some of them have even succeeded in representing him fully and in a praiseworthy manner.

Among them we mention Niki Foufa, Eleni Antoniadi, Maria Dogani (deceased), Eleni Kossifidou, Eleni Tsatsu, Anna Giavashi, Eleni Mavraki, Giannis Sgouros,

Soula Pouliashi, Kostas Dimelis, Pinelopi Kaklea, and others.

Furthermore, Andreas and Kallia, the biological children of the Master N. Margioris deserve special praise, since, as the natural heirs of his 189 works they took great pains, and continue to do so, to ensure their continued republication and to preserve and promote this immense written treasure of the Master with the cooperation and the help of his students.

Finally, I owe **permanent thanks** and **boundless gratitude** to my beloved Master and contemporary Greek Mystic **Nikolaos Margioris** for the endless hours of apprenticeship, the private teachings, but also for his tolerance of the incessant questions that I had the privilege of badgering him with continuously, for the numerous and profoundly multifaceted answers that he open-handedly offered me during all those years of apprenticeship, but also for the great burden of the responsibility that he reserved for me with the Inauguration of my School, the **Omakoio of Trikala,** in 1992, and for appointing me to represent his philosophical-spiritual and practical work and its propagation in Greece and abroad.

WHAT ESOTERICISM IS

Esotericism constitutes the most ancient **transcendental Philosophic System.** It is the emanation of the **esoteric** and **spiritual experiences of the Great Mystics**

of humanity, **men** and **women**, who left their personal mark through their high spiritual works that constituted **diachronic MODELS of superior thought** and **values**, of creative reflection, of consistent and complete **answers** and of **guidance** on the deeper **existential**, **ontological** and **cosmogonic matters**.

On the basis of the above, Esotericism examines and instructs on the **Roots** of **Truth**, hoping that, apart from providing a responsible **Esoteric Education**, it will give all the necessary **practical means** for every interested fellow human to achieve self-actualization, to **Know Thyself**.

In other words, along with the examination, study and teaching of the unmanifest laws that rule life and Creation, the communication with and the recognition of our **esoteric Self** is of essence in its highest expression, which is the attainment of the **Divine**.

Some of the most important branches of Esotericism that are taught in STANDARD esoteric scientific form are the following: Meditation, Esoteric Therapeutics, Esoteric Initiation, Esoteric Philosophy, Hypnotism-Orthopsychism, Scientific Spiritualism, Astrology-Astrosophy, Desymbolism, Ancient Mysteries, Antediluvian Civilizations, Philosophy of Yoga as a whole and its practical paths, Occultism (Occultology), Mysticism, etc.

ESOTERICISM FOR ALL

Laitsa Papandreou, the wife of Master **N. Margioris**, was the first one who had the inspiration of promoting

Popularized Metaphysics (Popularized Esotericism), which was printed on the title page of the first writings that Master N. Margioris published. Thereafter, he himself changed it to **Esotericism For All** and since then it has remained so, and the task of providing a substantial, deep but comprehensible **Esoteric Education** that will appeal **To All people** regardless of attributes, position, role, colour, profession or level of education was served as much by him and his wife as by all his students and staff without discrimination but with special zeal and self-denial.

THE MEANING OF THE WORD OMAKOIO

The word **Omakoio** is a composite of the word *omou*, (together) we hear. So, it means we hear highly **Esoteric-Spiritual teachings** (*hearing om* means we hear the perfect sound of OM).

The **Omakoio** was first established by **Pythagoras**, the Greek Mystic, in the middle of the 6th century BC, in **Croton** of **Southern Italy** and constituted the first real school of mass initiation to the exoteric and, especially, the Esoteric Truth of its time but also, in general, in the history of ancient and modern Greece – Europe – the West, while, at the same time, it laid the proper didactic and philosophical foundations for the incarnation of the Divine Word of **Jesus Christ**.

Nikolaos A. Margioris, the Greek spiritual Master (1913-1993), established his own School in **Athens** in

1976 under the same name **(Omakoio of Athens)**; then came the schools in **Lamia** (1990) and in **Trikala** (1992). He wrote more than **180 revelatory esoteric-philosophic and practical books** with profound analyses on various subjects and he left a huge, diachronic body of work for study and exploitation.

The **Omakoios of Trikala** and **Thessaloniki** have been actively teaching for **twenty-three years** while at the same time making their presence known by promoting the distribution of the **189 books** of Master N. Margioris and the **publication of books** and **essays** with many of the oral teachings and the profound views of **Nikolaos Margioris**, as experienced and transcribed by **Ilias Katsiampas**, a **student for over a decade, an instructor and a partner**, responsible for the above **publications and schools**.

After the transmigration of Master N. Margioris, more Omakoios were established in different areas of Greece.

WHAT A MYSTIC IS.
WHAT A MYSTICIST IS.
WHAT AN OCCULTIST-OCCULTOLOGIST IS.

Mystic (or Avatar, see the philosophical dictionary with Sanskrit that is in our first book titled *From the Master's Mouth to the Student's Ear*) means an accomplished and perfect spiritual-soul being who has been released from karma and rebirth long ago and is on a mission. As such, this being is incarnated in the world of matter as a simple and ordinary person and is, in essence, subjected to all the inflictions, the obligations, the duties, the obstacles and the human physical, familial, professional and social limitations that all of us are. More rarely, this being materializes temporarily in order to carry out an urgent duty and dematerializes again soon after.

In principle, a mystic is considered to be any evolved being that has been released from karma and rebirth. However, no matter how rarely this happens, it does not cease to be the beginning of the presence of a mystic and, at the same time, the "acme" of evolution of every incarnated human being. It is the first real step towards spiritual completion that, however, few people succeed in achieving.

Finally, the true and accomplished mystic is **only** he who knows **all** the inner worlds-dimensions of Creation and the beings that live in them **and** who **ALSO** faced, met, communed and united with the **Divine Presence** from here, our little planet earth. Or more simply, he comes to earth as such a being already formed and reconfirms, at some point in his life, all these Divine Rights he already possesses. Or, finally, for the first time, he slides and falls from **Occultism (or Occultology or Metaphysics)** and **Multiplicity** (the learning-study of the entire order of the esoteric worlds-dimensions, of the beings who live within them, of the unmanifest laws of Creation and the touching of the soul) to **Mysticism** (an individualized spirit similar to the Divine Spirit) and then to **Unity-Oneness** (One Truth-Source of Everything-Divinity).

Therefore, such a **rare Mystic-Messenger-Avatar** does not become, **he is Born**, fully formed by Creation. He is Creation... itself and the... Divine and its expression, as far as possible in our earthly world.

Except for on rare occasions, the Mystic remains in the discreet semi-darkness; though wherever he may stand, he irradiates the highest vibration of the Uniting Love, of Divine Justice and the Truth of the One Life.

Indicative examples of **Great Mystics of humanity**,

according to Édouard Schuré, who in his book by the title *The Great Initiates*, traces, registers, analyses and presents their superior life and their high superhuman and spiritual works, are, among others, always according to **Schuré**, the following: **Rama, Krishna, Plato, Hermes Trismegistus (thrice-greatest), Moses, Pythagoras, Orpheus, Jesus Christ** and we could add, on the **Christian Side**, the **following names** (most of them are small or great **Mysticists** and not necessarily mystics, apart from certain exceptions):

Adamantius Origen the Christian (the third director of the Catechetical School of Alexandria and who, in essence, shaped Christian Theology, despite the fact that his views, based on his own experiences, were in favour of the reincarnation of the soul and the Reconciliation of all creatures. Unfortunately, they were kept concealed from common knowledge and they were banished from the Dogma. It is estimated that he wrote more than 5000 books and, obviously, he must be regarded as one of the religious mystics), Paul the Apostle, John the Apostle, Anthony the Great, Athanasius the Great, Saint Paul of Thebes, Pachomius, Gregory of Nyssa, Saint Basil the Great, Saint Patapios (who, according to Margioris, wrote the pseudo-work – mystical (mystic) documents –by Dionysius the Areopagite, the first bishop of Athens, and which Eriugena, the Irish head of the Palace School of Paris translated into Latin in 850 AD, thus introducing Greek Christian Mysticism to the West and begetting, among others,

Saint Teresa of Avila, Saint John of the Cross, Francis of Assisi, Loyola and a long list of western Mysticists (Mystics), who kept the Western Church alive, appearing as its lifeline, even though it burnt so many of them, including Giordano Bruno), Tzalaluddin Rumi, Al-Ghazali, Saint Gregory of Sinai, Gregory Palamas (of the Uncreated Light), Nicodemus the Hagiorite (secular name Nicholas Kallivrourtsis), Theophilos Kairis, Cosmas of Aetolia, Nectarios from Aegina, Augustine, Saint John of the Cross, Nikolaos A. Margioris, and others.

On the **Philosophical Side**, we indicatively cite the following names: The Master of Ancient Wisdom (Ancient of the Times) or Djwal Khul or the Fourth Wise Man or the prefigure of Christ, Babaji, Sankara, Akhenaten, Saint-Germain, Homer, Hesiod, Pythagoras, Plato, Socrates, Plutarch, Heraclitus, Ammonius Saccas, Plotinus, Porphyry, Proclus, Chiron the Centaur, Asclepius, Trophonius, Iapetos, Prometheus, Sarpedon, Aeacus, Minos, Rhadamanthus, Apollonius of Tyana, Paracelsus, Alessandro Cagliostro, Ramakrishna, Vivekananda, Sathya Sai Baba, Nikolaos A. Margioris, and others.

A **Mystic** is the **occultologist-metaphysicist** who, at some rare moment, after many efforts and infinite suffering from the numerous incarnations, manages to attain perfection and change into a **Mysticist** – from one who is knowledgeable about the "whole" of Creation to one who is knowledgeable about the Divine (Knower of the Divine).

Then the knowledge of all the apocryphal worlds or of all the esoteric dimensions of Creation and of the beings that live within them is combined with the **Source of All**. Within him, Multiplicity becomes one with Unity-the Divine Unit and from then on he himself becomes a manifest or concealed **Man-God Protype** on Earth, either in the foreground or, as usually happens, in the background, always according to the special mission he has undertaken, fully cognizant of a **Divine Plan**.

It is clear that it is impossible to list all the important names that we could include under the word Mystic, and so we confine ourselves to mentioning the most indicative and especially important ones in order to provide the basic spiritual models of these people whom the rest of us, who are in the process of evolving, should pay special attention to, focus on and aspire to emulate. We should be inspired by their **Wisdom** and the **Model of Life** they provide for us DIACHRONIC-ALLY and which they invite us to adopt-follow-apply.

Furthermore, the **Truly Greatest Mystics** as **complete Man-God Protypes** are estimated to be between seven to twelve dominant spirit-souls – Words (Logoi) that are at times incarnated in order to attract and to set an example for humanity in evolution, by freely and always with self-denial and self-sacrifice offering the **Full Truth**, through the personal example of their own life, even going so far as to suffer crucifixion. Of these Mystics, only very few, you can count them on one hand, are usually incarnated and, of course, when they are alive, they remain unknown to most people.

Now, let's turn our attention to **Occultism and Occultology**. First of all, the term **Occultology** means **words about the occult and the analysis-presentation of the occult** in contrast to **Occultism**, which hides and obstinately keeps any knowledge it acquires for itself.

Margioris' view on these names that characterize those who occupy themselves with the **Metaphysical Sciences** is the following:

Occultists (occultism) are those that keep all apocryphal or mystic knowledge they acquire exclusively for themselves and do not disseminate it outwards. In other words, whoever remains secretive, non-communicative and unforthcoming with the esoteric knowledge he acquires belongs to the domain of Occultism and is an Occultist.

In contrast, **Occultologists (Occultology)** are those people (and that esoteric science) that gradually try to disseminate all knowledge they acquire in any way possible to their fellowmen so that they can use it, learn from it, benefit from it and make the most of it for their own evolution.

This is the basic but, at the same time, the most fundamental distinction between these two terms that Margioris distinguishes between in his philosophical-metaphysical work.

There are occultologists or occultists whose knowledge is limited to the etheric, the astral or even the lower intellectual world. They are the majority. In addition, there are others, superior beings, who exceed this order of things and reach the highest conceptual world (here they are definitively released from the burden of Karma and Reincarnation and at the same time they get a foretaste of mysticism; they are also called the newly appeared-small mystics). The highest occultists-mystics begin from the inner dimension, the Buddhic (10th), and can reach the 8th (the well-known Akashic Records of Creation are found here) or even the 7th Dimension, being the outermost border of Occultology.

From the 6th Spiritual Dimension to the Seat of the Divine, we see the beginning of Pure Mysticism that abolishes every trace of occultological knowledge and experience and puts the One Indivisible Truth of God in its place.

Finally, the **Mysticist (and Mysticism)** is the direct line of communication between a man incarnate in matter (spirit-soul) and God Himself or one of His rare and unique Aspirants. No other intermediate state of Creation can satisfy and fulfil the supporter-devotee of mysticism but its ultimate form, which is the Progenitor of All, who is God Himself.

Here we have two types of Mysticists: Those who come from Occultology-Occultism, who have gradually ascended and got a taste of all the intermediate worlds, have been satiated with experience, and, at one point, are entitled to become a Mystic; and those who, directly, without any previous contact with the intermediate worlds-dimensions, enter and experience the domain of mysticism.

In the **first case**, we have the rare occurrence that brings forth the **real Mystics** who have fully fused within themselves the relative-conventional truth of the worlds and of the beings with the absolute Truth of God.

The **second case** is the more common occurrence which includes most **Mysticists**, who, however, know almost nothing about the intermediate worlds and their function but only about the Nature, the Countenance and the Function of the Creator.

All of this will become more comprehensible to you after you read the following chapters about the structure of Creation and the layering of the dimensions, separating the Creator and the creatures and the chosen beings that minister to His Divine Plan. This distinction was deemed necessary so that each of us could appreciate the sheer scale of Creation and the essence of things, according to the mystics. In this way, it is easier for everybody to make comparisons about what one is served in one's environment and to have a set of criteria to discern that which is of higher and greater value in one's surroundings.

There are, of course, at least **three basic avenues in Mysticism** (see our book *The Apocalypse of John as Explained by Master Nikolaos A. Margioris*): **Religious Mysticism** (Christocentric and Christocratic

Mysticism and Bhakti Yoga of the Hindus), **Philosophic Mysticism** (Raja and Kundalini Yoga) and **Gnostic Mysticism** (Karma and Gnani Yoga).

ACTIVITIES OF THE OMAKOIOS OF TRIKALA AND THESSALONIKI ESOTERIC PHILOSOPHY, YOGA AND SHIATSU

Whoever wishes for information on **subjects, publications** and **the teachings of Esoteric-Metaphysical Philosophy, Esoteric Therapeutics** (Shiatsu, Finger-tapping, Static Therapeutics, ancient Greek Asclepiad Massage, glossotherapy, sleep therapy, or otherwise, hypnotism, and many others), **Yoga Systems** (Kriya Yoga, Yoga for kids, Karma, Gnani, Raja, Bhakti, Kundalini-Sahaza Yoga), **Atmoliquefaction** (a practical system for Weight loss, Detoxification and Slimming – N. Margioris' invention, based on the knowledge and on the practices of Yoga), **Gnosticism, Hypnotism-Orthopsychism, Scientific Spiritualism, Esoteric Initiation, Meditation, Esoteric Theology, Astrology-Astrosophy, Desymbolism,** etc., may visit our site (www.omakoio.gr or https://omakoio.blogspot.com) or contact us for more information.

- **We have** about **189 specialized books** that were written as a result of the **profound personal Experience** of Nikolaos A. Margioris, the contemporary **neopythagorean Greek Philosopher and christocentric mystic** (1913-1993), as well as about **15 books** that were written by his student **Ilias Katsiampas**, responsible for the **Omakoios of Trikala** and **Thessaloniki**, and president of the **Yoga Academy of Nikolaos Margioris – Omakoio**.

- On our website (www.omakoio.gr), you can see and order (eventually through Amazon as well) **any** of the nearly **200 books** you may be interested in, **relevant articles**, the **teaching activities** we offer (**lessons, seminars, speeches**), as well as **our annual programs**.

- Also, **seven branches** of **Esotericism** are offered as correspondence courses, with **30-33 lessons** each that have been prepared by Master **Nikolaos Margioris**. The branches offered are: **Meditation, Hypnotism-Orthopsychism, Scientific Spiritualism, Esoteric Philosophy, Esoteric Initiation, Astrology-Astrosophy, Esoteric Therapeutics and Desymbolism**. Ask for the relevant information booklets. There is a one-time enrolment fee of **10 Euro** for one or more branches and every lesson-triad costs **15 Euro**.

- **49 issues** of the purely **metaphysical magazine** *Omakoio* with well-documented articles. For the time

being, it comes out in Greek, in 8 hexads, at **25 euro** per hexad.
Please don't hesitate to request information booklets about all our activities. Analytical information can also be found on our website: www.omakoio.gr.
E-mails: omakoio@omakoio.gr or omakoio@gmail.com

Communication
Ilias Katsiampas
Omakoio
21 Kefallinias street, 42131 Tikala, Greece
Telephone and Fax: 0030-24310-75505 or mobile: 0030-6974-580768

Website: http://www.omakoio.gr
or https://omakoio.blogspot.com
E-mails: omakoio@omakoio.gr
or omakoio@gmail.com
Facebook Name: Ilias Katsiampas
or/and Ellie Katsiampas
Twitter: Ilias Katsiampas:
https://twitter.com/Katsiampas
Windows Live Messenger:
HLIAS: omakoio@hotmail.com
SKYPE: ellieellie59

NIKOLAOS A. MARGIORIS, THE SPIRITUAL MASTER AND CONTEMPORARY GREEK MYSTIC

Nikolaos Margioris was a contemporary Greek experiential neo-pythagorean and neo-platonic metaphysical Master, founder of the **Omakoios of Athens, Lamia** and **Trikala** and a **christocentric and christocratic Mysticist** and **Mystic**.

Within **23** years (1970-1993), he wrote **189 esoteric, practical** and **spiritual books** and taught the **Esoteric Truth** in Greece for **35 consecutive years** (1958-1993), using all the necessary practical means to make it accessible.

N. Margioris' teaching consists of the **harmonic coexistence** of **ancient Greek, Egyptian** and **Hindu mysteries** with the **inner Christian tradition.** Mainly, though, it is vetted, revived and crowned with **his** deep **esoteric** and **Mystical actualization** that contributes to the "treasury" of the spirit, and with **his personal**

Revelation, that is, his own **unprecedented experiential testimony** about the **Theogony, Cosmogony, Ontogony** and **Eschatology** of Creation.

He first established the **Omakoio of Athens** in Greece in **1976** in honour of **Pythagoras** and in order to revive Pythagorean views.

In the autumn of **1990**, he inaugurated the **Omakoio of Lamia**, run by his students **Dimitris and Koula Tsapara**, and in **January 1992** the **Omakoio of Trikala**, run by his student **Ilias Katsiampas**.

After his transmigration, in 1993, the establishment of more **Omakoios** around Greece followed, among which we note down the **Omakoio of Thessaloniki**, the **Pythagorean Omakoio**, the **Omakoio of Loutraki-Corinth, Comotini, Piraeus, Corfu, Rhodes, Karditsa** and **Glyfada**.

The **Omakoios** of Master N. Margioris constitute **autonomous, self-contained** and **independent Schools** of study in **Esotericism** (Occultology and Mysticism), **Yoga Systems** and methods of **Esoteric Therapeutics**. At the same time, relations between them are governed by the **Pythagorean Union**

Relevant **Presentations of** – **Extensive Dedications** to **N. Margioris** have been published in the magazine *Avaton* (issue of September - October **2002**); in the magazine *Third Eye* (issues of December **1992**, September **1993** and May **2004**); in the special supplement magazine *Phenomena* of the daily newspaper *Eleftheros Typos* with a nationwide circulation; in the magazine *Yoga* (issues of October **2008** and January **2009**); on **websites;** in **interviews;** in **books** of many other writers, students and others.

Specifically, in the December 1992 issue of the magazine *Third Eye*, he was characterized as the **Patriarch of contemporary Greek Metaphysical Philosophy** in an interview that he granted a few months before his physical death.

In a similar presentation in *Avaton* magazine (October – November 2002 issue) by his student Ilias Katsiampas, and within the framework of dedications to **Greek Mystics**, the magazine characterized him as a **Christocentric Mystic**.

Note also that in **February 2009, Nikolaos Margioris** emerged as the **60th** among the **100 Greatest (Leading) Greeks of all times** according to the results of an **open vote to the public** conducted in April 2008 by the Greek **television channel SKAI**.

Footage portraying the 100 people that were elected was broadcast by the television channel on the **16th and 23rd of February, 2009. DVDs** of the four-hour broadcast were also circulated. At the same time, the newspaper *Kathimerini* issued a **three-volume publication** with the 100 Great Mystics, which included a relatively analytical presentation of N. Margioris' life and work written by his student **Ilias Katsiampas** with additional information that was given by his son **Andreas Margioris**, professor of endocrinology.

Apart from his **cogitative** and **rare written work**, he left behind an **IMMENSE** and **diachronic – revelatory wealth** of oral spiritual testimonies on the entire spectrum of **Esoteric Philosophy** and **Mysticism – Theosis**, which, were they to be captured into the written word, would surpass the number of books estimated to have been written by Adamantius Origen.

The bright and multidimensional work of N. Margioris constitutes a priceless **Esoteric GEM – CHAPTER** of the greatest value for **Greece** and for the **World**, from one of the great spiritual children of modern Greece, who will undoubtedly remain in its history, internationally renowned and remembered for his benevolence.

INTRODUCTION

Any book that manages to contribute with deep analyses and clear answers to matters that have to do with the meaning of life and of the true purpose governing it is, by nature, important, interesting and catalytic for the decoding of a Superior Reality that is behind every phenomenon, supervising it, taking care of it and guiding it.

This is even more true when this book is the result and the fruit of systematic and fully controlled transcendental experiences of a few of our fellowmen, who have come to fulfil EVERY exoteric, esoteric and spiritual need of any person interested.

So, following this line of **transcendental instruction** and the **synthesis** – as far as possible – **of this multifaceted** and **infinite superior knowledge**, according to subject as well as a **panoramic-total appreciation of the WHOLE**, this book aims to contribute to this endeavour, by delivering in written form as many of the **VIEWS** of **these Great Spirits of Humanity.**

These unique beings of high spiritual value accompanied man from the beginning of creation, still accompany and will continue to do so, and functioned and function as **Guideposts** for his safe navigation through the **matrix of matter, the... etheric and... hyper-etheric world, so** that he can find not only the balance and the conventional harmony in the world of contrasts where he lives, but also the direction of the evolution he deserves, his true destination toward the gradual likeness of Divine Perfection from which everything derives and... ends...

This may or may not be done by any incarnated spirit-soul either by taking the firm decision to pursue its initiation and accelerate its evolution by following in the footsteps of the Mystics of the human race, or by following the vaguer and more sluggish progress that is determined by the pace of the slow and step-by-step evolution of a large part of humanity. Otherwise, what prevails is the indifference of several incarnated souls (followers of Antithesis-Satan-Matter) towards the Divine Plan – or their opposition to it –, which may lead to their incarnation and reincarnation, and make them utterly dependent on Matter-Antithesis and the heavy karma they create until the ... **End of Time** (the final closure-the end of the whole of Creation that will happen after ...billions of years), which will mean the forced and violent separation – with the greatest and never-ending pain – from matter and all the external and internal parts of the soul, until its complete liberation from all the shackles and forms it donned, served and regarded as the only existent truths and necessities from which it is now freed, not voluntarily and smoothly, but through the Divine Providence-Command, since the whole of Creation (exoteric and esoteric) is withdrawing-dissolving-deconstructing. And all the tardy and protesting souls gather simultaneously, suddenly and inexorably, with whatever this may imply in regards to the successive pain caused by the destruction of the flesh and the violent death of all external and internal forms taken by these souls that are attached to matter (coarse and fine) and rebelling against evolution.

The freedom of the souls lasts up to this point, before the End of Time brings the restoration of the Divine Order and ... their self-enlightenment... through the now Inescapable Divine Grace for all the remaining "lost" sheep.

In the person and the work of **Nikolaos A. Margioris**, the contemporary Greek Mystic (1913-1993), there are infinite oral and written testimonies that encompass his truly personal experiences concerning the entire spectrum of the **esoteric** and **spiritual perception** of **human** and **Divine Life**, and **ANY person** can take those elements that his idiosyncrasy, his psychosynthesis, his interests, his choices and his karmic needs dictate so as to point him in the right direction in his relevant search.

Recognizing the need for **substantial answers** on all

the basic existential, ontological, cosmogonic and eschatological matters, we thought it would be useful to present a series of introductory and well-documented writings that are based on the profound spiritual work of N. Margioris and of many other Great Spiritual Beings in order to responsibly and reliably guide whoever seeks deeper and more substantial answers to all that concerns him as an individual and as a spiritual being.

After our first introductory book with the title *From the Master's Mouth to the Student's Ear, with a thorough philosophical dictionary of Sanskrit of 400 words for the students of Yoga* that circulated on Amazon in digital and printed form, and the second book with the title *The Apocalypse of John as Explained by Master Nikolaos A. Margioris*, we now present our third book with the title *The Mystery of Death and the Post-Mortem Course of the Soul*.

Our ambition is to publish, at some later time, the only book worldwide about **Life After Death** by our Master Nikolaos Margioris, which, for the first time, publicly, analytically and fully explains **ALL** the stages of the post-mortem course of the soul of every man, the **ENTIRE** range of the esoteric dimensions of Creation and the role of the evolving spirit-soul which, with the completion of its spiritual evolution, becomes able to reach the **Divine Side** of the **Father** Himself (The Unapproachable Light of the Father).

It is a work like no other, a deeply personal, experiential, visionary, revelatory work – as is his other book, *The Birth and Death of the Worlds and the Beings, Matter – Antimatter – Hyper-matter, Universe – Anti-universe – Hyper-Universe –* that constitutes a unique spiritual MILESTONE of revelation, grounded in hyper-substantial Ontogonic, Cosmogonic and Eschatologic analytical descriptions and extensive transcendental analyses of personal experiences.

CLARIFICATION

We remind the reader that what he is holding in his hands is a metaphysical text whose purpose it is to inform, as far as possible, about delicate, sensitive and elusive matters which most of us have not managed to become familiar with or which we have simply set aside and basically, with few exceptions, deal with only when we personally happen to face our own matters of death, either of family, friends, acquaintances or when we ourselves or people close to us encounter death.

That's when we realize that not only are we not equipped to deal with this event, which no one escapes, but we feel at a total loss because due to ignorance or shallow knowledge, we feel that everything "ends" with death.

We may get a partial, general answer on the matter of death from different sources and other registered events that occur around us daily, in hospitals, in homes, on the road, in the countryside, where some people pass the threshold of death and return to narrate their experiences to us.

But the special, extensive, analytical and complete answer has been given, since the very ancient years, by the **experiential metaphysics** of the **mystics** and of the **spiritual Masters** who **they themselves** or their **students** narrate or write to us about, in unbelievable detail, the entire process of transmigration and especially of the invisible events, locations, dimensions, situations, movements, courses and the continuation of the soul to other invisible worlds, which by divine order and justice is inimitable and inconceivable to human common sense.

This **Metaphysical Perception** will parade itself throughout this present book from beginning to end, so we are obliged to inform and to warn the reader that he must be prepared and he must realize that we will enter deeper scepticisms and transcendental situations with which the reader may scarcely, if at all, be acquainted with and he must be patient and persist in completing the study of the book before he reaches any conclusions.

PREFACE

Having observed local and international publishing activities during these last few decades, one notices that there has been a great publishing boom of books which focus on the mysteries of life and ancient civilizations, on yoga, on alternative-esoteric therapeutics, on the subconscious as a medium, on extra-terrestrial intelligence and its possible presence on earth, as well as on the esoteric and spiritual search and actualization of man.

This is evidence of a steadily growing interest in everything arcane and that many people feel a vital need to receive answers to crucial and imperative questions as well as a personal practical confirmation on many such matters.

With this plethora of **information** and **misinformation**, which, in essence, is somehow metaphysical in hue and content, an unbiased and attentive student will ascertain rather easily a commercialisation of the esoteric-metaphysical sector, which often leads to the glossing over and embellishment of many issues set forth in order to make them more attractive and easier to sell. For they satisfy the affective and egocentric elements of every individual, and in fact, in a rather pathetic, receptive, self-serving manner (without any real Guide-Master), without any real evolutionary progress required. Evolution is portrayed as a reward... an attribution of justice ...from armchair critics... for the action or the... expectations... the blessings of different earthly, or even extra-terrestrial, vessels of our times... who offer crucial help ... from high above (superior help) for the ascension... a kind of massive evolution of humanity, in fact... that is lying ahead... and will soon be upon us.

All these scenarios, which seem to be dominant of late, have gradually led to an indirect or direct detachment or deviation from the **Genuine Experiential Metaphysical Knowledge of the Mystics.**

That is to say, beside the **Pure Metaphysical Knowledge of the Mystics, another type of knowledge** has been flourishing for a while now. This knowledge differs greatly from, and in some cases even clearly goes against, the metaphysical perception that advocates the **personal responsibility and action of every soul** for himself and others, but also the absolute need for a **responsible earthly Guide-Master.**

This is clearly seen by the fact that anything arcane, extra-terrestrial or metaphysical that appears is accompanied, in many cases, by an arbitrary and continuously modified calendar date promising the salvation, or the spiritual rising, or the spiritualization in general or to a great degree of the human race.

Such reports present humanity as already having attained a high level of evolution and readiness; this readiness is presented with beautiful sounding messages and with a given course... a neat transformation of the human race due to positive energies that... are arriving....

The promise of the coming of a cloud of photons is good... for instance ... but the Truth and Metaphysical Realism are better. No cloud of photons – like the one that many people expected to arrive (2012-2013) and change humanity – is enough to catalytically change ANY individual who has not ALREADY, on his own initiative, embarked on the **esoteric transformation of himself**, and has not devoted plenty of **personal time** and made **objective sacrifices** in his daily life for his necessary transformation, always with the guidance of and in close cooperation-apprenticeship with a **suitable Spiritual Master.**

Everyone receives, if he receives anything at all, what he deserves and what he understands; that is, what his PRESENT evolution allows him to understand. Everything else is a glossing-over, an idealization as well as an escape from the karmic duties of each individual.

It is one thing to talk about a general move, improvement, a new starting point for the potential evolution of humanity, and quite another to talk about individual acts which are justly connected with the quality of the evolution of every soul and the real or not real steps that one takes toward one's esoteric or spiritual ascent.

Of course, if we believe that the effect of these events corresponds to today's General and Individual Evolution of Humanity and of each of us, and, in fact, without our making the slightest implicit or explicit effort, offering or sacrifice for the whole, well then ... *"we should act fast!"*

We avoid referring to scenarios of **mass... and... rapid or direct ascent** of people to the fifth or sixth dimension, which many choose to serve en masse nowadays. With their unconventional terminology, with the way they are presented and with what they profess, we believe that they have deviated from the Pure Experiential Metaphysics of the Mystics. Please carefully consider what I have told you and what I will tell you later on, and judge for yourselves.

In addition, we have the "expedient interventions", for example, extra-terrestrials in the service of terrestrials, as if everything were settled, as if there is no individual responsibility for one's evolution, no individual or collective karma and individual and collective settlement-payment (on condition that we do not continue to acquire new karmic debts, something which clearly happens, and it is just as clear that to fulfil one's Karmic obligations within the framework of an incarnation constitutes a small part of the total karma that every soul carries in its bag).

All this occurs when, although there is great interest on behalf of our fellowmen, there doesn't seem to be a real understanding of Metaphysics nor a substantial shouldering of personal responsibility in each person's life, and the life of humanity.

It is quite clear that nowadays we are going through an unprecedented general karmic slump (see extensive comments in the prologue and epilogue of the bilingual Greek-English book *The Apocalypse of John as Explained by Master Nikolaos A. Margioris, with extensive prologue and epilogue analyses-comments by his student Ilias Katsiampas*. It is available on Amazon and other electronic means), and this for one proves, if nothing else, how imprudently we have behaved towards each other, as well as towards the animate and inanimate life-nature.

Therefore, there are **no** benchmarks for evolutionary advancement **nor** even basic esoteric ones, **but** there is a standard of a necessary balance-settlement of our accumulated and numerous ominous karmic obligations on a universal level that we must endure ... settle, equate.

Whether we will be able to overcome this worthily or not is another story that cannot be foretold by anything but the evolutionary choices and the current existent or non-existent level of evolution of the incarnated souls, which appear somewhat immature and slightly unevolved ... regardless of arguments to the contrary and the visible phenomenon of a general and broader tendency of humanity towards esotericism (not spirituality, that is too often confused with esotericism).

Let us take a look around us, as well as within ourselves, and let us judge accordingly. Here, it is **necessary** to mention the existence of the **spiritual Masters** as well as of the **Mystics** of **Humanity**, who are the **ONLY ONES ABOVE karma** and who, for thousands of years and to this day, have **SHED LIGHT** on the ascending path leading to the **Spirit** and the **sacrifices** required.

Terrestrial and extra-terrestrial beings, whatever type of exoteric or esoteric evolution they may have, either upwards or downwards, or in both directions at the same time, are all in the same "boat" concerning good and bad karma and the slight inclination in one direction. That is the truth whether we like it or not.

Those who make the difference in these two... camps (terrestrial and extra-terrestrial) are only the very few **INCARNATED Mystics** (terrestrial and extra-terrestrial) wherever and however many of them exist, and the few **incarnated spiritual Masters** (we also call them **hyper-terrestrial beings**, firstly, in order to distinguish them from other terrestrial and extra-terrestrial beings, and secondly because they are the only real **and fully-conscious members of a Celestial Hierarchy** who are incarnated on earth or on other planets on a mission), recently freed from karma, who responsibly guide souls (of terrestrial and extra-terrestrial beings).

And behind them and mainly through them, the

real esoteric and spiritual help of Universal Value and Substance comes **only** from the **hyper-terrestrial** (discarnate beings of the Celestial-Spiritual Hierarchy) who are materially responsible for the actualization of a **Divine Plan** of which the **REAL Servants-Workers** are **ONLY** the **incarnated MYSTICS** and **to a minimal extent** the incarnated **spiritual Masters** and the **Mysticists**. All the others, **without exception**, apart from the very few rare cases where students of theirs are deemed able to execute the work on themselves and on their fellowmen reliably, lack the guaranteed esoteric insight and more particularly, the spirituality required.

Even the people who are vividly interested in Metaphysics and the works of the Mystics-Spiritual Masters, and not in the works of the other karma-burdened individuals who unsolicitedly represent metaphysics, in essence avoid applying what they've learned in their own life and have only a few evanescent moments of genuine efforts to respond to superior inducements and even fewer instances of applying them to evolution. As for the rest of our fellowmen, they are dragged along and go wherever the winds of exoteric and esoteric desires take them and satisfy them... **karmically and materialistically.**

Please, admire any good extra-terrestrial beings; "cooperate" with them if you can, if you are sure of their intentions and their agendas (or even the agendas of terrestrial beings who appear as extra-terrestrial beings or as communicants with them) and if you have the ability to perceive them; but don't become over-awed by the number of years (which could be in the thousands or millions) of technocratic evolution before us, or even by the little esoteric evolution (not spiritual), and by the flood of messages and the promises they make that appear to have come from extra-terrestrials, or perhaps, by the pious hopes or needs of fellowmen acting as mediums who proclaim them as messages of great value, and which may be genuine or distorted or fake.

That is the path of evolution we are on and at times, as souls, we become carriers of an earthly physical body or an extra-terrestrial one...

For more analytical information, see N. Margioris' book, *The Other View of Erich Von Daniken's Dogma, Terrestrial, Extra-terrestrial and Hyper-terrestrial Beings* and others.

May we all be able to perceive and distinguish what is of value from among the gallimaufry of human vanity, from among the voluntary or involuntary peddling of hope (or the voluntary or involuntary disinformation) that we will become the centre of the world, semi-knowledgeable and with a pseudo-perception that is artfully cultivated as a spirituality that will come almost exclusively extra-terrestrially (or from the superior clouds of photons or directly from the celestial hierarchy through some... communicants or mediums who supposedly bring us into contact with "our superior selves" or with "discarnate masters" of the celestial hierarchy or from alleged masters who "raise" us... spiritually).

And in fact, **only the MYSTICS** possess **this spirituality and it** constitutes the **final destination** (after the difficult struggles of many victorious incarnations and with the successful disposal of karmic burdens) of every evolution of the souls from the terrestrial, subterrestrial and extra-terrestrial grounds-origins that are altered and upgraded, from bad, mediocre, good, better to the few mystics who touch upon perfection-spirituality-the god-man protype.

May the above approach somehow play a role in encouraging a purer **esoteric** and **mainly spiritual distinction for those** interested in the real evolution and not what is offered bountifully nowadays and distributed far and wide ... or with a calendar promissory note ... that ... is continually renewed.

Above all, search for **EARTHLY spiritual Masters** and/or **Mystics**, or at least consult their **Extant works** (old and new) or any former students of theirs so you can gain a clearer picture of the Truth – exoteric, esoteric and spiritual – on any said matter, whatever its origin.

Finally, in order for us to form a **PANORAMA of life and evolution** that is more compatible with the exoteric, esoteric and spiritual truth within ourselves; one that will basically **demand** and **require** our **active cognitive participation** and that we **RID OURSELVES** of every **material** as well as **etheric** (gas) and **astral bond** (delusions, fixations, stagnation, karma) with which we have been surrounded and equated with or which our other karma-bearing fellowmen have presented to us as a prerequisite or an expedient outlet.

Good luck to us/you....

This mostly invented knowledge of human origin or, if you like, this mixture of knowledge, has long gone by the name of **light metaphysics or para-metaphysics – para-spirituality.** It is so called because it does not agree, to a large extent, with the **basics** and the **roots** of the **Metaphysical Science of the Mystics**, and quite often, it blatantly disregards them, proposing its own set of human and exoteric (or mildly esoteric) principles, which may or may not be disguised as material needs and satisfactions about matters that are purely or dominantly Metaphysical or even Spiritual.

There is a **Need to Turn** to the **Pure Metaphysics of the Mystics.** Away from, or rather ABOVE the combinations and amalgamations, human, commercial or even purposeful deception or the obfuscation of the true destination, and the true individual and collective opportunities and obligations of every person in our world.

This, of course, can only happen if the elementary-introductory knowledge, the direct testimonies of the mystics of humanity – the only ones with the mission to deliver the Perfect Models of Truth on all matters of the present and the other life – is made known and taught alongside all other partial or invented human knowledge.

Only in this way will every man-soul be given the opportunity to gain true insight and to compose, with greater ease, the truths of Life and Creation and to become more **deeply** and **substantially equipped** to **compare** and **distinguish** between the human and the spiritual, the false and the real, the mortal and the eternal, the imperfect and the perfect and to avoid any deceptive or falsely embellished pseudo-presentations or partial knowledge of little value with which they try to win us over and draw our attention, and which, in many cases, may distract us from the **Great Spiritual Truths** as well as from the **true practical ways of evolution** that rightly guide us towards them.

In any event, a person who has all the evidence before him will decide what is right and wrong about the matter plaguing him, and he will take a stand in the eternal battle between good and evil, between the superior and the inferior, between the imperfect and the perfect. This will also mark the assumption of personal responsibility as concerns the karma that belongs to him, his fellowmen, creation, the soul-spirit and the Divine Truth.

THE BASIC STRUCTURE OF OUR WORLD ACCORDING TO THE EXPERIENTIAL METAPHYSICAL VIEW

As a whole, the Universe or the World is not only what we can perceive with our physical eyes or with the help of the most sophisticated conventional and electronic equipment, such as telescopes – microscopes – cyclotrons, which are at our disposal at present or will be in the future.

What we see in the **celestial-macrocosm** and the **sub-atomic cosmos-microcosm** using all the modern means is, of course, not the entire physical-material Universe. In fact, we are in no position to know, with precision, the undefined extent of its expansion into Chaos.

According to more recent **Cosmological Scientific Knowledge-Discoveries, 4% of the Universe** is the **visible-perceivable matter** with **all its individualized** and **partial differentiations** as we perceive it all around us with our five senses.

23% constitutes **Dark Matter** that remains unexplored and unperceived by all of us, and the remaining **73%** consists of the thoroughly unknown **Dark Energy**.

It is certain that this unknown **96%** will hinder developments in **scientific knowledge** for an **indefinite period of time**, whatever its speed of progress may be... At the same time, this **96%** and **especially** the **1000 per mille**... that science has yet to **touch upon and which** comprised, comprises and will comprise the **permanent presence and SUPREMACY** of **the invisible tiered gradation of the Esoteric Worlds of Creation** that leads to the **Creator Himself**.

So, it's quite **OBVIOUS** that what we **know** – **comprehend** and **dare** to say that we **grasp**... is literally a **drop** in the **Ocean of the hyper-dimensional OCEAN** of the...vast **ESODEPTH**.

We should also add that this **96%** of **amazing** and **unexplored area** – and even the **one thousand per mille** or even **more** of the **UNKNOWN** – consists of an infinite body of knowledge, values, esoteric laws, revelations and grounding of **Esoteric Knowledge (Occult – Metaphysical)** whose higher levels or **highest peaks** are **gradually conquered** by **the most deserving of our fellowmen (Mystics)** who have either fully realized or are now beginning to realize that they belong to the world of **Experiential Metaphysical Truth** and that they must **make** some of their experiences known for the **benefit** of their **fellowmen, as a** somewhat disguised inspirational gift of **keys – instructions – points of reference for the scientists** who are following a different and **very slow path of advancement and approach** the **Esodepth** (as incredible as it may appear at present, given our earthly findings) from the outside inwards, in **contrast to** the **Metaphysicists** who observe things from the inside outwards.

From the **Source** to the ultimate end of Creation and the Beings that evolve within it. From the **core** of the **Life of Everything** that we call **God** to the outer region where we all find ourselves and move around with total freedom of thought, word and deed.

Naturally, that is also how **Evolution** occurs (exoteric and especially esoteric, and more rarely spiritual). It **is supported** and **guided** by the **core** of **Creation**, based on a **Divine Plan**, created by that **Hyper-Intelligent Entity** we call **GOD**, who as an **All-Seeing Eye** with its **extensive uncreated RAYS**, offers **spiritual values** and **revelations** of **His Laws for the good of all** through the **few deserving** and **highly-deserving of our fellowmen** in order that **they themselves** and **the more mature** souls **can be guided** to the **same redeeming experiences** that all of humanity will sooner or later be guided to. This humanity with its numerous, unripe still incarnated souls will follow more slowly, more heavily on a longer and more **arduous karma-burdened** course against the **few already mature** or even the **few who, of their own free will, are fully aligned** with the **truths** of God and of His Creation.

So, according to the Great and Divine Beings-Mystics of Creation as well as to the latest findings in Cosmology and Nuclear Quantum Physics, the present matter-morphic Universe, known and unknown, despite its deceptive conventional infinity is, in fact, an infinitesimal fragment of the Divine invisible Universe of the multidimensional graded Esodepth – Eso-dimensions of the WHOLE of Creation.

Now, if we wish to see the basic principles of the structure of our World and Creation through the eyes of an **accomplished Mystic** who experienced **Multiplicity** and **Unity** and who fully connected them within him, we should make some mention of the following:

According to the great Mystics of humanity and in particular according to the work of **Nikolaos Margioris**, the contemporary Mystic (as stated in his books *The Birth and Death of the Worlds and the Beings (matter-antimatter-hypermatter, universe-antiuniverse- hyperuniverse), Life After Death, Esoteric Philosophy* and others), after his last repose (Sanskrit *Pralaya*), the Creator moulded a new Creation out of His Divine Centre – Divine Matrix; a new Creation Radiating outwards.

This radial breath of creation formed **thirteen (13) Divine Establishing Rays** that used their Energy to form the **thirteen (13) separate and independent Creations – Universes**, every one of whose **Rays** manifested **thirteen(13) distinct Dimensions**. In fact, **each one of these Dimensions** consists of **seven (7) sub-dimensions**.

We (our earth and our physical-material universe) belong to the **7th Establishing Ray** from the total of the thirteen (13) that concern the Universes and counting from the inside outwards, from the spirit to matter. We are in the **13th outermost Physical-etheric Dimension of our world** (1st Spiritual, 2nd Spiritual, 3rd Spiritual, 4th Spiritual, 5th Spiritual, 6th Spiritual, 7th Enadic – Divine (Adi), 8th Monadic (Anupadaka – Akashic Archives), 9th Nirvanic – Atmic, 10th Buddhic – Intuitive, 11th Mental Lower and Higher, 12th Astral – Emotional, 13th our own Physical-Etheric Dimension, and the 14th (which is in the process of being formed that we don't take into account) with its seven (7) sub-dimensions. This means that there are twelve (12) more dimensions further in with the respective seven sub-dimensions of every dimension.

In sum, we have **thirteen (13) Main Dimensions** with their **seven (7) sub-dimensions – sub-levels** in the **7th Establishing Ray** which totals ninety-one (91) sub-dimensions throughout the entire construction of the specific 7th Establishing Ray to which we belong and in which we live, function and... evolve at its outermost and most matter-morphic points.

The first six (6) Dimensions are purely spiritual and the remaining seven (7) may have a small or large percentage of material connection, material participation. The higher and more inward one of the seven Dimensions is, the faster, higher, more supremely and more perfectly does it vibrate. The lower and more outward bound a Dimension is, the more of its initial speed does it lose and its pulse-vibration continuously slows down until it reaches our physical world where everything stands still, crystallizes and vibrationally freezes, presenting us with its matter-form.

Our physical-etheric world (13th Dimension) has seven (7) sub-dimensions. Three-sevenths (3/7ths) are made up of the three known states of matter: solid, liquid and gas, and the four-sevenths (4/7ths) are made up of the etheric-invisible side of matter that also has four states of finer and faster vibrating matter that makes it invisible in the physical side of our world, which we call etheric matter.

This etheric matter lies behind physical matter since it constitutes the matrix, the mould, the prototype on which physical matter-form is built.

Whatever exists in our physical world represents an invisible esoteric matrix of production. First, there is the creation of the etheric prototype of every morphic representation, and then the physical-morphic replica follows.

There is nothing in nature, matter, form, the world, that does not have its original form in the etheric world. That's why our world is called physical-etheric; because there is a definite close relationship of continuous cooperation and ceaseless interaction.

The Energy of Life (Prana) comes from the etheric world and it ends up supplying the physical world with life, shaping the morphic presentations and preserving the coherence of the links that connect animate and inanimate matter.

With this short account of the Divine Acts, we **only make reference to** the creation of the **13 Worlds-Dimensions-Universes** (through the relevant **13 Establishing Rays** that emanate from the Divine Mind) with their 13 Dimensions for every Universe separately and, of course, the seven sub-dimensions of every one of the main 13 Dimensions. So, the Universe with Its 13 Establishing Rays and the 13 dimensions of every Establishing Ray provides 169 Dimensions in total with their respective sub-dimensions (13 Establishing Rays × 13 Dimensions – Worlds = 169 Dimensions – Universes. Still 169 Universes – Dimensions multiplied by 7 Sub-dimensions of every Dimension – Universe = 1183 sub-dimensions).

At this point, we shall not refer to the Creation of the **Anti-universes**, nor to the **Chaos**, and definitely not to the **Hyper-universes.** These constitute three other, independent and autonomous parts of the Creation of Divine Reality with their own roles and purposes, which, in some cases, are involved in the evolution of souls that come from the Universes.

But these form a separate and specialized chapter that we will not occupy ourselves with in the present work as it strays far from our own small problems that govern our life as well as the events that accompany it between life and death and during its ascending evolution, and which concern all of us within the framework of the ascending scale of the dimensions that comprise the 7th Establishing Ray to which we belong.

And all these events take place between the physical-etheric world (13th Dimension) and the astral-emotional world (12th Dimension), but they sometimes, though rarely, reach the lower mental dimension (11th Dimension).

This is the arena within which the evolution of the low, middle and little advanced incarnated and karma-bearing human beings takes place and, always of their own free will and with the freedom to pursue their materialistic choices and identifications with which they continuously interact to build a strong or weak relationship of dependence with matter, from which they rarely manage to entirely free themselves.

Metaphysics attempts to deeply enlighten man about all this, to properly instruct him about life and its destination and the practical ways with which he can wean himself of his dependence and regain the full spiritual freedom of his soul.

Then we can say that this man philosophizes profoundly on the meaning of life and begins to explore the mysteries of the worlds, of the beings and the Creator himself. In the eyes of the other people, he will appear as a person with characteristics of a moral or holy man, because he will cease to behave in a lowly manner and will, in fact, exhibit high morals and superior thoughts and behaviour.

This man builds his lower and higher mental body

and rapidly heads towards his release from Karma and the obligatory rebirths. He is the victor of life and death. Because he manages to go beyond them, to release and recognize the divine qualities and powers that he possesses within himself, and which remain crystallized for as long as he is dominated by material desires.

So, he comes even closer to His Creator and His Divine Wills and begins to partake more and more of the Divine Knowledge, the Divine Blessedness and Bliss and to work in order to instil these values in the other, uninformed, limited and still enslaved human souls.

SPIRIT, SOUL, INTELLECT, MIND, BODY

According to the Metaphysical Truth of the Mystics, man is a composite and multidimensional being. He has an individualized spirit and soul (in a word, we call them spirit-souls, since they constitute an integrated reality, as we shall explain below), forty-nine (49) carriers-vestments-bodies that it receives from the matter of every dimension – sub-dimension through which it passes during its descent and depending on the minds it forms.

More specifically, every man (terrestrial or extraterrestrial) incarnated in matter, regardless of the basic constituents of the matter that surrounds his body (carbon, silicon), bears the spirit and soul within him in the 13th Dimension of the 7th Establishing Ray in which we find ourselves.

The individualized human spirit is a direct product of the Divine Spirit; it is an invisible crumb of the Divine Bread of His Life, of the Substance of His

Hyper-substance, which can **NEVER** deteriorate or change or be lost. Consequently, it has the same divine and imperishable attributes of immortality and eternity that the Creator himself bequeathed to it.

When, as an individualized spirit, and after its initial divine birth, it begins its first detachment from the home of the Creator in order to tour and to explore the created Worlds-Dimensions below (initially the six spiritual ones) it moves in the full glory and knowledge of its divine origin as a spirit between the 1st and 6th Spiritual Dimensions of the 7th Establishing Ray.

However, when it wants to get a closer look at the lower regions of Creation (from the 7th Dimension to the 13th), the objectified – dual side of the creation of the Creator, then it is destined to pass the first barrier, the first station-border that separates the upper Worlds-Dimensions from those below, from absolute perfection to moderate perfection to ... imperfection.

From the frontiers of the 6th Dimension, it will pass into the 7th Dimension. But because the individualized spirit is an unaltered part of and consubstantial with the perfection of the Divine Perfection of God, it cannot and must not enter the nether worlds unprotected, and it must not be infected by small and large percentages of material participation contained in the creation of the nether worlds.

Its perfection must be protected with special armour. For this reason, the exact moment it crosses from the 6th into the 7th Dimension, when the slight and least material participation begins, the spirit emits an energy from within, a spiritual substance from its own being, which combines with the matter of the 7th Dimension and covers it protectively, forming an impenetrable suit of armour, a spiritual membrane that is called the **soul**.

The soul inherits all the divine attributes of the spirit, as well as the main responsibility of governing the vessel with its many additional plates of armour that it will wear as it descends from every Dimension and sub-dimension separately and from which it must pass in order to reach the ultimate end of our world (13th Physical-etheric Dimension).

The spirit supplies the soul at the moment of its birth with 103 hyper-senses, hyper-attributes that accompany it throughout its entire descent and, in particular, throughout its ascending journey, when it has finally broken free of the matter-form and it awakens some of these divine properties.

The spirit is now represented by the soul that assumes huge responsibilities and numerous missions.

The primary role of the soul in the outer-lower worlds of the 7th Establishing Ray essentially begins from the 7th Dimension and reaches the 13th Physical-etheric Dimension, where it will at some point find itself descending and passing through all the intermediate Dimensions and sub-dimensions.

From the **7th** to the **13th Dimension** we have **seven (7) Dimensions** in total (7th Enadic -Divine (Adi), 8th Monadic (Anupadaka – Akashic Archives), 9th Nirvanic

– Atmic, 10th Buddhic, 11th Mental Lower and Superior, 12th Astral – Emotional, 13th our own Physical-etheric Dimension).

Each of these seven (7) Dimensions has seven (7) sub-dimensions. So, we have seven (7) Dimensions ×7 Sub-dimensions = **49 sub-dimensions**. The soul is in charge of governing these seven (7) exoteric Dimensions with their respective seven (7) Sub-dimensions, that is 49 sub-dimensions-worlds.

That's its responsibility and its role. To govern all these vessels, protective suits, armour that it wears on its voluntary descent – its submergence into the nether worlds. From every world – dimension that it passes through, it is obliged to form the relevant vessel and sub-vessel from the matter of the dimensions it enters so as to be able to manifest itself in it and to interact with it. At the same time, it forms the respective minds.

Every vessel that the soul wears on its descent is all the heavier and denser, vibrating more slowly, and giving rise to its desire to acquaint itself with the world it is passing through. But when the soul descends to the nether worlds for the first time, it follows a steady descent into the astral world (12th Dimension) where it makes its first stop to prepare for the final destination, so that it can, at any given moment, be ready to enter the etheric and physical world that constitutes the last station of arrival-incarnation and the gaining of experience.

In metaphysical terms, this entire process is called

Involution (descent, fall of the soul to the nether worlds or original sin) and is continued-accomplished with its incarnation in our physical world. That is, the soul continues its plunge into the physical world by surrendering to it.

As soon as it has donned its last etheric protective suit, and has incarnated into the body of a man, of a newborn infant, the consciousness of the soul is immediately erased and lost (marginalized) and responsibility for this newly arrived physical vessel is handed over to the mind of the external coating of this physical man.

When the new Mind assumes power over this new physical carrier, made of the same materials plus the fine materials of the physical world, the new ordeals of the soul (spirit-soul) begin.

As soon as it awakens, it is already drunk on the wine of matter that it so recklessly drank in with its new mind and the five senses it has acquired. The lust to learn about the lowliest area of pan-creation, the physical-etheric, begins.

Thousands of desires flood and overwhelm it, sweeping it further and further away from every distant memory of the great presentations and high status of the spirit. It creates a strong and increasingly growing attraction for matter and "its joys"; it slides into it and fully surrenders to the need to satisfy all its desires and passions.

In our daily life, the soul compels our senses to collect experiences from the innumerable antitheses of our physical-etheric world. Every image is conveyed to the **soul** through the mind and then through the **intellect** that is the finest material tool found above the Mind, until the full maturation of the unripe Mind is complete.

The soul accepts and embraces the mental image with motherly love, it dresses it in ectoplasm, it looks after it with unbelievable care, and when it is certain of its beauty, it sends it off to its inner spirit. This waits with its 1003 gates, or entrances, or reception points to attract and to absorb the mental images attracted by the soul.

However, most of the times, the spirit, due to its nature of perfection, doesn't accept any of the psychic images sent and returns them to the soul, which in turn gets upset, becomes embarrassed, concerned, irritated, frustrated and traumatized – hurt.

And that is how repression occurs; and in order for it to live, it does harm in two ways. First, it consumes the soul's psychic liquid (prana) in order to survive; and secondly, it obliges the soul to force the senses to produce similar images and so, the repression expands and dominates the freedom of the soul.

Repression then enslaves the soul and buries it in too many incarnations. It belongs now to the sensual dynasty – side – location. And that is the tragedy of the soul.

In its material drunkenness, it forgets its mission and it is not at all interested in its inner spirit. The internal warning bells ringing within as the voice of conscience, reminding the soul to return to its initial obligations, have no effect.

The soul sneers at these voices of conscience and tries to do the opposite to satisfy its material trysts. Thus begins its tragedy and its comedy. It fights against the spirit and it obediently follows the orders of matter for long time periods of incarnation.

While deep down it is immortal and eternal, it seeks the inexistent, vain, material treasures. It is the soul's time of delusion and tragedy.

A long period of falling and getting up again intervenes before the soul reaches a state of saturation and material asphyxiation that makes it turn full force towards its spiritual centre. Toward its spiritual restoration. Or, in other words, to acquire the sufficient amount of experience and prudence that comes as a result of the seasoning of the soul through the many reincarnations and the blows from Karma that the soul itself provoked with its thoughts, words and actions.

Upon initiation of its restoration, it hears the bell of the spirit and feels ecstatic and dumfounded. It immediately grasps what is happening and senses the drama. The first regrets begin to surface and its thought begin to focus more and more, and increasingly more steadily, on the spiritual ascent-return-meeting.

Little by little, it starts to forget all previous events and it begins seeing them in the proper, esoteric light. It looks up and perceives the consecutive regressions and descents, and it calls out, 'Yes spirit, regain your soul.'

From this moment on, a new, more superior and worthier orientation begins, which guides man toward the ability to commune with the soul and the spirit using his mind and to take from here, from our earth, everything that rightfully belongs to him and has been given to him by the Divine Spirit, thus dominating over matter and Creation and becoming a grounding conductor for Celestial Reality and Divine Freedom.

Only with the above knowledge can we gradually enter, and improve and more deeply understand the great issues of our times and of all times of humanity, but mainly the childish promises some people make concerning easy paths of ascent towards the spirit, with ascensions in supposed fourth, fifth and sixth dimensions (as if it were the end or an amazing event or an easy and... collective achievement) which are actually right next to us (etheric, astral and mental world) and set strict conditions and demands for the true release and deliverance of the soul from the vices of Karma and reincarnation.

Ascension is very different from what is implied or distortedly portrayed by different voices and is dominantly an issue-conquest of the great spiritual Masters and Mystics, and certainly not of every superficial, credulous individual or even of those considered experts on metaphysical matters, or several typical esoteric and initiation experiences our fellowmen have with the dimensions that are close to us. These people know nothing about the ascension in general, let alone the collective ascension of our fellowmen in our times.

Now, we are called upon to examine, in depth, the great subject of the recycling of life that is continually repeated with the phenomenon of death and rebirth in the great school of matter.

THE MYSTERY OF DEATH AND THE POST-MORTEM COURSE OF THE SOUL

The present book examines the great and everlasting question of life after death. It is a profound and detailed study of the subject of death that is based on the experiences of great spirits of Humanity, and mainly on the testimony of revealed knowledge and the personal experiences of **Nikolaos Margioris**, the contemporary Greek philosopher and mystic, writer of more than **180 metaphysical and practical books** and a teacher of an **immense spiritual legacy** he left behind.

Throughout this book, we will be accompanied by the esoteric experiential truth of life with its own soul-spiritual means: with the eyes of the sixth sense, of the soul and of the spirit. Along with these, clairvoyance, intuition, out-of-body experiences of the soul and of the spirit that go by various names (Samadhi, Theosis) and that occur throughout the whole spectrum of esoteric Creation, will play a dominant role in our narration. However, we will focus on the phenomenon of post-mortem life, its stages, the pathogenic states of the departed souls as well as of the ones left behind, the basic dimensions that the average human soul will pass through, the regions where it is said to be found, and every possible detail that may be of some value. They may be of some value either to those of our fellowmen who are examining the question of post-mortem life for the first time, or for those who are expanding an already existent body of information and knowledge they may have built from different sources.

Post-mortem life is an exceptionally interesting topic and always relevant for those who are alive. Because the others seem to have lost interest as they don't expect nor await the phase of death. For all of us, the apparently living, the subject of death is always pertinent and relevant. And we can say with certainty that, generally speaking, there has been no person on Earth, throughout the ages and the centuries, who has not wondered, speculated, introspected – secretly or openly – about the matter/subject of death.

Without exception, all people throughout all the ages have raised the question of what happens after death and if there is life after death. And again throughout all these ages, answers and theories concerning the phenomenon of death have been suggested either as isolated explanations or as part of broader philosophical, religious and other trends.

First of all, let us start by saying that it is improbable that we live a whole life, which we estimate at about one hundred years, and that suddenly, a sword swings, the guillotine falls, and this life ends, losing all continuity and destroying whatever man might have made, produced, created and formed during this lifetime.

The conception that everything ends with death is quite vain and childish. It is quite narrow-minded and limited in its capacity to provide concrete answers and, in all cases, renders the life of any person meaningless.

So, in this sense, a death, and every death of a person, appears to be a predestined end although it is not exactly definite when it will come; just predestined from the beginning, from the moment of one's birth.

Therefore, whoever is born is destined to follow the law of death. But despite all this, everything one experienced and everything one created has a purpose. Otherwise, we must accept that everything happens for no reason. Everything occurs without purpose, without reason, without potential, without cause. Everything happens just to happen and there is no ulterior purpose, no reason to hoard experiences for later use.

And so, we arrive at a very materialistic conclusion; a conclusion that is very limited, very extroverted, very humble and which states that we are what we eat, what we drink and what we breathe. Hence, the descent of morality. The degradation of man. The decline of man's potential. Man has no destination. It is the abasement of whatever may be of a deeper essence, permanence and value in man. And that is, more or less, though disguised, the view of the materialists, of those people – who even in our days when nearly everything has been overturned – still believe that it is matter that plays the primary role in life.

In brief, they believe that matter is the underlying power of life and of the presence of beings and of everything in the Universe. Needless to say, this doesn't hold. And it hasn't held true scientifically either for many years now, regardless of the fact that science still does not have a universal perception of things. Though it can't be denied that in the past few decades, science has cultivated a hyper-metaphysical perception and it has shown that the underlying cause of the Universe is not the physical structure of matter but that there is another primitive state and cause to be found "above matter and beyond space and place."

This cause is the **First Power of Life or the Liquid or the Water of Life** (Prana for the Hindus, Holy Spirit for the Christians, Entelechy for Aristotle and Basil the Great, Eternal Fire for Heraclitus, Energy for Science, Substance of Life for the ancient Greeks and many others) that emanates directly from the **Creator** and is responsible for the creation, constitution, coherence, maintenance and the continuous replenishment of matter, of any matter with life – the physical as much as the "non-physical" (immaterial or etheric, astral, mental, etc.).

In juxtaposition, we have the opposing position, the

materialistic theory stating that we are material beings, and we are born, and we will die, and that there is nothing after death, and everything goes back to where it was produced. So, everything is lost. Memories, events, experiences, souls – everything. Of course, as long as some people survive us, they will remember us and keep our memory alive, but that's as far as it goes.

But the above views debase and degrade the status of man and the Creation of God, who is governed with INCREDIBLE CAUSALITY AND INCREDIBLE INTELLECT, and turns him into a random being who acts in a mechanical way. A person is viewed as having little value and being of low quality, as if there is no intelligence, as if there is no Intelligent Causal and Supervising Principle for EVERYTHING. But for all that, we still want equality among the people. For all that, we still want morality to exist, but in a very conventional way. We want it to be materialistically centred, possessive in essence, that will prove inadequate when called upon to keep the balance between societies, people and external life.

On the other hand, we have, all the great religious currents and mythologies of peoples – of all peoples without discrimination – from the very ancient years. And of course, we also have the philosophies and mainly the esoteric philosophies that are hyper-metaphysical.

They are suited to give answers. And they give their answers open-handedly. Some in a more dogmatic and absolute way; that is, in a somehow authoritarian way, as in the case of religious dogmas which say: that's how things are and there is no room for discussion nor the need for well-founded explanations on the subject. In other words, it is a matter of faith.

Then there are the others, the philosophical currents and mythology. Mythology explains things indirectly, through symbolisms, parables, narrations that represent the entire course of man between life and death, and many other issues. And we either understand them or we don't.

There is also **Philosophy**, and in particular **Esoteric Philosophy**, which, with the salvaged **transcendental experiences** of the great Masters, Mystics and Guides of humanity, comes to shed the **Highest Lights** on the Truth about Life and Death.

And as we are closer to this approach – without exempting any other because they are all of value but we simply cannot enter into discussion about all of them – we will suffice ourselves to at least discuss the **Christian Religion** that concerns us more, since a large part of humanity happens to be Christian.

It is well known that Jesus Christ spoke of the Kingdom of the Heavens, of a Heavenly Kingdom that starts from within us and remains deep within us. *The Kingdom of God is within us.*

He spoke of a Kingdom that man had to prove worthy of conquering. And he must, from that moment on, commune and participate within it. From that moment on, his presence in life is within this Divine Kingdom that will bring him near God. He even said, with the deep parables of his time, that *"in My Father's house are many mansions"* (that is, many dimensions). Therefore, we are talking about degrees of ascent and perfection of the human soul.

All the great religions – **Hinduism, Buddhism** and others, without exception – refer to the subject of life after death and have answered with absolute certainty in the affirmative. However, they haven't done so generally and vaguely, but by creating immense philosophical constructs that man still labours to assimilate as knowledge, due to their immensity and their complexity and to the great amount of time one needs to devote to studying and comprehending them.

Nevertheless, there are introductory books that can help us and give us a concise overview of all that we need to know in order to arrive at the first basic answers following a sound and well-grounded route.

So, **death**, according to the **Metaphysical perception of things**, is a door. It is a necessary transition man must go through from the visible to the invisible presence. Because, if, according to metaphysics, religion and anything having to do with mythology and philosophy, man has a **permanent nucleus of life** within him that touches upon **eternity** and what we call God, with whom he is constantly connected to, then this eternal nucleus of life cannot be corroded or altered and certainly not destroyed.

So, what do we mean when we say death, metaphysically speaking? We mean that the time will come when a person who is born and ages, has completed his cycle organically, materially, as matter, as a physical carrier, as a physical body, as an organism, and having fulfilled the course he was meant to fulfil, he comes to a physical end.

In other words, the body ages. Its bodily functions gradually deteriorate and it reaches a state of no return. This doesn't mean that this procedure cannot deviate or occur suddenly.

There are many cases where an accident or a suicide, a sudden event or something unexpected cuts the thread of life of a person before he matures and ages naturally, reaching the point of accepting, in essence, the fact that death must come.

And yet, it does not always arrive then. That is, during the full maturity and aging of a person. It may arrive much earlier, uninvited and without warning. Basically, death arrives unbidden and inescapably. That is why, in the New Testament, Jesus says that we must work as if we were to die tomorrow. The next moment. The next day. Because, if we don't do so, we don't fully fulfil our duty nor do we improve our position and our evolution. What's more, we don't display the necessary readiness for evolution and, at the same time, we fall short of the interest and support of our fellowmen.

These are basic values and do not randomly come

out of the mouth of Jesus Christ. We must be at the ready as if we will die immediately after. This means that we must have settled things in our life as much as possible. For example, issues concerning inheritances, family, friends, humanity, society or other matters should be dealt with.

We must have settled issues that have to do with our daily life as much as possible. But above all, above the human, the professional, the social, and all the others, we must have settled the affairs of our **soul**. Because if we don't have a settled soul, whatever else we may have settled, we will have somehow failed a test and our course will be questionable in terms of the metaphysical perception of things.

More or less, we have all experienced the death of people in our immediate or broader environment. A death always seems to be something harsh. Something that causes pain, something that actually contains pain within it. And, in fact, this pain is often immense and unbearable.

In other words, we have one person who is losing another person who is very close to him in a violent and abrupt way, throwing the former into a state of shock because he could not believe that death would knock on his door, would take a person close to him, a person with whom he might be connected psychically more or less. And the more connected someone is with this beloved person, the greater the pain that comes with death. It is a pain that is double.

First, for the person who is leaving and "is gone forever" and **second** and **more important,** and this is true in most cases, for the one who stays behind. What will become of me now that I have lost my loved one? In other words, because of the psychic and the closely egoistic connection between people, our reaction is adverse and completely negative, which is, however, a human factor that one cannot eliminate in an automatic way...which means that this pain must be experienced, within measure.

So, the face of death appears to be and is harsh. It often comes without warning and brings us to our knees. It takes us by surprise and it fills us with feelings of confusion, anxiety, pain; it causes conflict and reactive behaviours towards others, to the dead, to ourselves and to the one we call God.

And so we have a very particular situation in which the phenomenon of death naturally occurs. Or, if you wish, unnaturally, though everything is normal, but we simply cannot perceive it and follow it as normal, due to our limited and imperfect ability to conceive events through our five senses, which only capture a range of things in the world, in this world of the physical vibration of matter. They cannot capture the other one – the one that is superior, invisible, etheric, energetic – even though it evidently exists.

Nobody knows when he will leave this world. Only the Mystics know that. And some Great Masters who are given notice before they depart, so that they may be cognizant of it and have time to "pack their luggage".

Of course, the soul of every person knows when it will leave and tries, by using the appropriate means, to pass the message on to the mind (consciousness), which is quite obtuse and cannot comprehend. That's why some subconscious stimuli end up guiding man, involuntarily, toward an unconscious preparation for his departure from this world.

So, the soul knows; besides, it's the soul that gives or executes the karmic order to actualize the phenomenon of death. However, it simply cannot convey the expected to consciousness, because in the average person, there is no communication between the soul and consciousness. The soul sends some stimuli to the subconscious, which in turn conveys-directs them as much as possible to consciousness as nudges to settle affairs, to conclude various pending matters. These messages are not always heeded because they aren't always fully perceived by consciousness, but only partially so, or as much as is karmically permissible in each individual case.

Therefore, the soul of every person not only knows the exact day when it will leave the body, but it has the absolute responsibility of actualizing death. Consciousness doesn't know it. The subconscious receives this information indirectly and tries to prepare consciousness and its close friends and relatives.

Apart from this, a death means an interruption of

life. Interruption of life means that a person loses his physical presence as an incarnated soul in a human body, which means he disconnects the soul from the body and cuts the energy cord that connects it. Disconnected from the body, the soul now permanently moves around in the adjacent etheric body, also called the energy body of man that rules and supplies the physical body with life; and so the physical body begins to waste away.

In other words, the organism now ceases to function. The heart stops beating, the internal secretions in the human body stop and its temperature falls and freezes until it becomes immobile. Macabre but real. We are describing it at this moment. It is a physical sequence of things in which, according to Esotericism as well as esoteric religious knowledge and other knowledge, **death** has seven **phases**, seven different and consecutive stages.

These stages differ from one case to another. That is, in some cases these seven stages may happen within a period of days, hours, minutes or seconds. It depends. Or even within months; you may have heard the phrase "his soul isn't departing or isn't leaving", often used for people who are dying from serious diseases but death doesn't come and they go through a heavy ordeal until it happens at some point. So, how quickly one goes through these seven stages differs from case to case, depending always on the personal karma of every soul.

But once the first stage gets underway, then the final countdown that will gradually, but inevitably, result in physical death begins. That is, the remaining stages will slowly begin to follow suit as the case may be. Let us note that every human body is of etheric and physical constitution. In other words, it is physical and etheric at the same time. Both physical and energetic.

We know its physical part because it is composed of solids, liquids and gases. We are not too clear on its energetic part but, so that we may have a picture of it, we present it as a bodiless, intertwined, fiery body, a body of cords of fire that governs our physical body and supplies it continually with life. Since life comes from within.

Imagine a net covering our whole body, a bright net through which a fire of life that we call Prana passes. We call it our Spiritual Life Force. We call it the Substance of Life. We call it Magnetism, Bio-energy. It goes by different names. Aristotle and Basil the Great called it entelechy. Pythagoras calls it Kind and Form or Kind of Form.

All these names refer to the **Divine Life Force** circulating in the etheric body and which supplies the physical body with life. Please note, the result, the sub-product of this Divine Life Force that runs through our body is the aura, which is transmitted and radiated out of our body. It is not the etheric body. See N. Margioris' book *Esoteric Therapeutics* that explains the esoteric anatomy and physiology of our physical-etheric body and their close cooperation and interconnection and their effect on the phenomenon of life and health or disease, the chakras and the precise physical glands they correspond to.

What's more, if we observed a person with the eyes of the soul, of the sixth sense (intuition), we would see that exactly above his head, there is an inverted cone over which flames continually appear like bolts of lightning, like blinding flashes of light stretching upwards and inwards toward the head.

This inverted cone or mushroom is an apparatus of etheric constitution and structure and in the Sanskrit language it is called **Sutratma** (see Ilias Katsiampas' book *From the Master's Mouth to the Student's Ear, in the glossary of Sanskrit of 400 words for the students of Yoga and Esotericism, available in the English language in digital and printed form from Amazon and other digital platforms*) and in the Christian terminology **The Silver Cord.**

To the **Mystics**, this structure changes form, composition and abilities and takes on a completely refined etheric-astral-intellectual and hyper-intellectual structure called **Antaskarana** (or... Antahkarana) in Sanskrit, and which now has the form of a **triple antenna** that rises in place of **Sutratma.** This triple antenna functions only **partially** in the **great spiritual Masters** (small mystics) and **fully** ONLY in the **GREAT Mystics (God-Man Protypes).** It functions in **nobody** else.

When someone recognizes the Sutratma for the first

time, he is bewildered and wonders what is happening. In fact, it is Prana entering the etheric brain of man through this inverted cone and it is distributed in the etheric energetic body in order to supply our etheric and physical organism with life.

So, when we say that a death takes place, it means that the soul closes this cone that lies on top of the head in an etheric state. This cone has a valve in its depth, on its base – a special etheric valve. This valve is ordered by the soul to turn and close when the moment comes for a person to die.

When we say that one has shuffled off this mortal coil or that one has drawn his last breath, it means that at that moment the soul is turning and closing this valve and so preventing the insertion of new Prana, new Substance of Life, new Life Force in the human body. We shall explain the causes later.

Automatically, the physical decay of the body begins due to a lack of the Substance of Life. In the second phase, the seven centres of power close. That is, the seven etheric glands, the energies, the chakras as they are called in the language of Yoga. They stop the supply of energy to the physical glands.

When the life force-power of the energy centres and of the Nadis close, so does the physical supply to the glands and the cells; to the physical glands, to the seven known ones: Pineal Gland, Pituitary Glands, Thyroid, Thymus, Pancreas, Genital Glands and Adrenal Glands. By closing the supply to the physical glands, they cease secreting hormones. Life ceases being generated and regenerated.

At the same time, before these procedures begin, a hormone is secreted from the head – and it is discharged only at that moment – and we call it in the language of Esotericism the **Death hormone** or the **hormone of Deliverance.** It is the hormone of the **end of life** that benumbs the human body in order that a person can pass on to death without suffering pain. It brings on a sweet narcosis.

As soon as this hormone, the death hormone, is secreted, the person relaxes and it is said that he is **angelized.** Do you know what that means? That his intuition begins to open. That is why many of our fellow humans who are present at this phase, beside someone who is ready to leave this world, notice – during the last hours or days – that this person suddenly loses contact with the environment and with those around him and seems to be communing with the beyond, with the nothing, with the air, with the after-world.

Or he starts to call out names of the deceased, as if they were close beside him, talking to them. This is a normal procedure, because at that moment he is beginning to have moments of clairvoyance. And he sees the souls coming as relatives, friends and acquaintances who are there to meet him on the other path of life, the CONTINUATION of life, the post-mortem part of life, the life that is invisible to the physical eyes.

After the closing of the etheric and physical glands,

there follows the natural procedure of the termination of the provision of life and the beginning of the deterioration of the human carrier. More specifically, the body begins to inhibit its functions, to end them and then the verified death we all know arrives.

So, death in **esoteric scientific terms** is when the continuous supply of the Essence of Life is prevented from normally entering the physical-etheric carrier of man.

After the phenomena mentioned above take place, we have the opening-awakening of Kundalini (stored spiritual energy – energy stored inside us in etheric state at the base of the spine, at the coccyx) which burns upwards and ejects the soul out of the body.

In other words, at that moment, the soul leaves, is disconnected from the body, the etheric umbilical cord is cut, the double frontal etheric tape that forcibly kept it within and continuously connected it to the physical-etheric body.

What is Kundalini? It is the coiled spiritual energetic force within man lying at the base of the spine (coccyx) but in the form of energy. It is created by the imported prana of seven composites/seven qualities and is gathered and stored in the coccyx in immaterial etheric form with exceptional dynamics and exceptional concentration, remaining dormant, frozen and permanently unused in the average person, with the exception being the Masters and the Mystics.

At that moment, it is released. Consequently, the soul

too departs. It must now find a way to escape-release itself. And there are at least four ways for the soul to escape-exit the body. But this is another specialized area of study, presupposing additional knowledge and several evolutions of the soul. Of course, after the exit of the soul, a course of gradual decomposition of the physical body ensues. That is, whatever is material will return to the material elements wherefrom it came.

Magnesium will join magnesium. Phosphorus will join phosphorus. The salt will go to salt and so forth. That is, the body will start undergoing its decomposition. Its ruin. Its destruction. The atomic matter of the body will go to the general Matter of Nature and the spirit will head toward the spirit, to the level it deserves based on its evolution. Consequently, this obligatory separation takes place.

The physical carrier is then lost but does not disappear immediately with the departure of the soul. Simply, a slow, reverse course begins whereby the body gradually deteriorates as it decomposes due to the lack of the Substance of Life. That is to say, the body faces its destruction.

If we follow the procedure of burial and not of cremation, this may take up to three or four or five years, depending also on the soil in which we are buried, as it is not of very good quality lately. So, matter returns to matter. It returns and becomes equivalent to the cause of production of the physical body. This concerns the physical part of man, which by nature and status is temporary and varies from incarnation to incarnation.

The energetic part of man, the immortal, the imperishable, in other words, the soul, the spirit, moves to the etheric body, which in turn, also must be cut into four pieces. That is to say, it too must gradually dissolve after the death of the physical body. There is a procedure whereby first the body dies and then comes the etheric death (it is also called the second death), so that there is absolute deliverance of the soul from these two bodies that restrict it, so that it can peacefully and freely head for the level of its own evolution – which it has accomplished in its life – usually for one of the seven steps, sub-dimensions, sub-levels of the astral world.

That is to say, whatever the soul, as an incarnated person, has accomplished regarding knowledge, regarding morality, regarding worth and merit, regarding whether one undertakes and fulfils their duty in life or not, determines where one is destined to go in the post-mortem phase of life, which is now invisible to the remaining physical beings.

But before this happens, death must have come to the physical body and the soul must have moved on to the etheric body that also has four layers, four states of matter, four layers of dimensions and must be dissolved before it can freely depart for its destination.

Because the physical body is governed by solids, liquids and gases. The etheric body is governed by four more states of a finer and faster vibrating matter than what we know with our five senses.

So, the etheric body must also be destroyed in order that the soul can freely go to the astral world, which is the world of desire that we have built from here, and stand on one of the seven sub-levels, sub-categories, steps, sub-dimensions that this world has.

They are vast areas, dimensions of separate and full existence. To be exact, they are sub-dimensions/sub-levels of the astral or emotional world, and each soul, with its respective structured astral body will find itself in one of the seven sub-dimensions to whose matter it corresponds.

And if we take them from the lower to the higher, we could say that the first two are those dimensions referred to as 'hell' in religions, because they have to do with souls that knowingly served evil during their lifetime. They consciously committed crimes. Whether planned and premeditated or impulsively, they committed criminal acts throughout their whole life. Therefore, their presence and actions were of a criminal nature.

This presence of people of a criminal nature in thought, deed, action and word will go to the **first astral step**. There, the soul will not receive punishment under coercive conditions by devils piercing them with tridents or simmering cauldrons and fire that popular religious tradition would have us believe, but it will suffer a type of self-punishment and compulsory self-consciousness, both in the first as well as in the second astral step, which is slightly more refined than the first, though the difference is small. Everything else about hell and demons that torture us are symbolic and form a part of popular beliefs whose aim it is to show the harshness of the self-punishment of every soul that will find itself there.

On the **second** step are those who changed a little for the better and who don't have evil on their mind night and day, but do add a little goodness to spice things up. The beginnings of goodness. Because this goodness is neither real nor absolute. They have begun to change their way of thinking slightly for the better and they have begun to acknowledge, to some degree, their previous wrongs. And only when this happens – which is difficult and rarely occurs – do they move from the first astral level to the second, but without having fully disconnected with evil, to which they still tend to lean, though they are no longer fully and continually dominated by it.

And we also have an example from the New Testament, from Lazarus whom Jesus resurrected, and whom he brought back from the other world after three days, and when the unhappy Lazarus returned, the first words he said were: *"I saw pains, I saw fears, I saw hard times and terrors of the heart, of the lips and don't ask me anymore. Give me some water so that I can wash off the sorrow."*

Those were Lazarus' words upon his return, and at

some point afterwards, he became a bishop and served the Christian religion and he always spoke of this experience he had, referring apparently to these first two lower astral steps, which are the filth and stench of man, the dregs of the souls of human society, the impenitent criminals of humanity.

The man came back and when narrating his experiences, he remembered all that had happened to him. The memory remained vivid. These images were so upsetting and shocking that they remained in his physical memory even after he was resurrected by Jesus.

So, we have these first two steps that the soul goes to – if it is so destined. Because the other souls that don't belong there evolutionally are, of course, better people during the course of their evolution and advance to the upper astral steps that correspond to their own phase of evolution.

Some souls are closed "buds", others are blossoms that have begun to open and others have a large flower. Every soul not only differs according to the work it did with itself, but also according to its relationships with its fellow humans.

Other souls go directly to the **third astral step**. Others go directly to the **fourth**. They pass with lightning speed through these worlds and you do not want me to describe these worlds (one will find detailed novel analyses for all these worlds in the book *Life After Death* by **Nikolaos Margioris**, the contemporary

Greek Mystic, which we soon hope to make available to you in the English language. (On our part, we have already translated it into English and have passed it on to N. Margioris' children for the final editing and promotion).

They go to the **fifth**, they go to the **sixth**, they go to the **seventh** astral step. And those who are nearly Masters or perceived as saints in religious terms, go to the first mental step of the mental world, to the second mental, to the third mental, to the fourth mental. And some of them, who, when they come back to earth are regarded as small or great envoys, go from the fifth mental step and above. They usually leave immediately. They don't even cast a glance behind them. They consider our dimension a fetid and filthy well, from which they managed to free themselves on their own merit and so they rapidly flee without looking back, like prisoners when they are released or when they manage to escape from the prisons where they are forcibly kept until they serve... their sentence.

Therefore, we have one category in which humanity as a whole – 90% of humanity and more – belongs and which is located somewhere between the first astral level and the seventh. The greater part of humanity belongs there. **Don't** make the mistake of thinking the largest part belongs to the mental level. Only some very evolved individuals, known as saints, or Masters – some widely recognized as such, others less so – or novice Masters belong there.

They are the ones who have partially comprehended-conquered life. They are the ones who can raise themselves above life and its vain ambitions. They are not affected by what is happening in life, although they interact within it in order to aid their fellowmen and to allow their own refined evolution to continue.

Their evolutionary course, with its many consecutive incarnations, has been long. They are considered old souls with vast and invaluable experience, with great knowledge, with wisdom, with the greatest distinction, with a refined sense of justice and with a value system that touches upon and serves what we call the **Divine Plan**.

In fact, they cooperate in an impressively harmonious and compatible way against all of the rest of us who, in essence, object, directly or indirectly, to this Divine Plan and for this reason we obstruct our evolution and that's why we suffer pain and anguish. For no other reason.

In any case, according to the metaphysical perception, death follows the course that corresponds to each individual's degree of evolution. The more mature, the more moral, the more accomplished individuals were during life, and the more serious their efforts at evolution, the higher they will find themselves on the astral steps, in the astral regions, and they will receive the corresponding privileges and rewards.

Because the rewards of the first and the second astral level, which are a type of compulsory self-punishment where the predator, the villain of yesteryear, becomes the victim of today. And he becomes the recipient of verbal abuse, he is taken to dark places, sunless areas where freezing winds blow and pierce the astral body of the soul of this specific first or second sub-dimension of the astral world.

Guilt and remorse eat away at him. And if they don't eat away at him, they certainly appear before him and in time, they create matters to occupy him and make him see what is happening, where he was at fault, how much he hurt others and what harm he caused them. He is made to suffer what he did unto others in the same way, with the same intensity and to the same degree until he realizes that these are exclusively his own mistakes, his own crimes, his own karma, his own choices and deeds which he committed in thought, word and deed against his fellowmen, so that he can gradually reach the point of full understanding and regret in these dark and sunless areas. The areas of ice-cold and etheric humidity, of extreme conditions and absolute and fair self-punishment.

Beings of the diaconate (angels or masters) don't make an appearance there; there is only a faint light when the new arrivals of the soul approach, and as soon as they appear, the little light that existed in these areas grows dimmer and absolute darkness that pierces the souls and the astral bodies of the beings there, prevails. This hell is worse than the hell described by Dante, for those who are acquainted with it.

And things are pretty much the same, a little less intense on the second step. But, from time to time, a faint light appears, especially when some of them have reached the stage of regret; this light is nothing other than the beings of the diaconate who serve there, coming to take them away. In other words, the angels of the religions come and take the SINCERELY repentant souls – because sincerity and insincerity are clearly distinguished here – and raise them to the next step, so that they can be incarnated again at some point or other so as to continue their evolution, or, after basic preparatory instruction, they are given the opportunity of a reincarnation.

Nothing is static; everything follows a dynamic continuous course of evolution and perfection of body and soul. The **dynamics** of the **evolution-perfection** of the soul is put in motion, however, exclusively within physical matter by every incarnated soul within it and is connected exclusively with its thoughts, its words and its actions throughout its entire physical life.

As for the other astral steps, the same thing as described above happens, only that the locations, the facts and the conditions greatly differ. More specifically, the average modern person who is simultaneously sometimes good and sometimes bad, who regresses and vacillates, begins at the **third astral step**. This person has not fully consolidated and established his evolution. Depending on the conditions, on life events, on personal interests, on his humble intentions and several other situations and... trials... he sometimes reacts calmly, with compassion and understanding, and at other times his reaction is awkward, spasmodic, aggressive, vindictive, etc.

He is the typical materialist who is more or less self-centred. A person who looks after his own interest, a person of necessity, a person with intentions and the tendency to exploit. Everyone understands what we mean. These people are on the third astral level, where there is not much darkness. But there is not much light either. It is an intermediate state.

From the **fourth astral step** and on we have a state that very much resembles human reality in that a large part of humanity belongs here and in the previous third astral step.

What we see more in the third astral step and less in the fourth is that people are willingly trained using their astral intellect to create whatever their mind and needs desire. A house, a garden, fields, animals, plants, the Planet earth, the universe, the world, everything...

In other words, people learn to operate their will and imagination. And with these two attributes they shape their creative potential, which is externalized in the fourth astral dimension with a virtual reality that resembles what they have experienced on Earth, and which they are called upon to reconstruct. Besides, the astral matter of the fourth sub-dimension of the astral world is not only exceptionally malleable and suitable for the creation and materialization of every human thought and interest, but also for the astral education that is provided by Masters who descend for this purpose.

Namely, they impose their will and their imagination and form similar conditions to what they are used to here on Earth, or they begin instruction on superior ways of thinking, emulating the standards set by the guides-teachers of the region.

The same thing happens, though on a more advanced level, on the **fifth astral path**. The **sixth** and the **seventh** are simply steps taken mainly by the initiated and our more accomplished fellowmen. The uninitiated cannot go there. And no one can climb another step if he doesn't truly deserve it, if it doesn't correspond to his current spiritual evolution and does not activate-awaken his corresponding astral body there. This requires a lot of work with oneself. And in order for this to happen, one must refine one's way of thinking and one's morality so that it corresponds with the astral step one is vibrationally suited for.

Otherwise, a person cannot enter because the vibration doesn't let him. It is a different vibration. It is a higher, faster vibration. He cannot get in because he has not created the corresponding astral body. He will remain outside and the moment will come for him to realize, to act and become worthy of it.

There is something else I must tell you about the sixth step that may help you understand some other things as well. There is something particular about this step because the sixth astral step contains a self-illuminating presence of light, which doesn't emanate from a single point or source, but by many. That is, it can be found throughout the entire being of this dimension simultaneously. In other words, there is a self-illuminating presence of light without a focal point. Light is emanated from everywhere.

And such is the unity of the light and the elation and the well-being it spreads in the souls that some who arrived there thought they had arrived in Paradise. And they took it for granted and, with persistence and dogmatism, they created heresies here on Earth. In other words, some who entered the sixth astral step while incarnated here on earth – without having died, of course – created new religions, new heresies and various other "forms and shadows" to glorify the Paradise they saw there, and which, we could say, under certain conditions in the future – peace and harmony and all those other higher sentiments the souls in their astral body experience there – could become a physical /mental reality for the already incarnated souls. Under certain conditions. When most incarnated souls on earth evolve to the corresponding and analogous level. Despite continuing to be present here on earth.

Of course, this will happen **only** when **a large percentage of people** reach a point of refined and higher evolution corresponding to this level. Something along the lines of a **Third Greek Universal Civilization**, which many say will arrive at some time in the future, to once again bestow, on a universal level this time, the Spiritual Lights on humanity.

As for the recycling of the peoples (reincarnated evolved souls) and the civilizations (roots-races), this happened many thousands of years ago (from about 16000BC to 18000BC), in the broader basin of the Mediterranean, during the time of the **Dravidians**, the ancestors of the **Pelasghi**, ancestors of the **Greeks** and foes of the Atlanteans (see Nikolaos Margioris' books *Dravidians, the Ancestors of the Greeks; The Reign of Minos, the Great King of Crete; The Desymbolism of Greek Mythology; The Eleusinian Mysteries* and others).

Different superior beings that don't necessarily come from human souls descend to or pass through the sixth astral level from time to time. These beings may be large angelic or archangelic beings or beings of the Celestial Hierarchy. Certain angelic beings are on a mission of descent or supervision on the lower steps.

On occasion, especially on the first, second and third astral step counting from the bottom up, from outwards inwards, from matter to spirit, only beings of the diaconate, whose duty it is to supervise the souls, may make an appearance.

On the upper steps, apart from beings of the diaconate, Masters may also slip in. Masters who come from the human race, incarnate or discarnate or also from species of parallel evolutions (seven of these are known to us, see the three-volume book by N.

Margioris titled *Occultology, The Two-Volume Metaphysical Encyclopaedia* and the magazine *Omakoio* with its 49 issues).

The Great Masters of the White Brotherhood often hold meetings on the seventh astral level. And whoever has reached the seventh astral level knows that several important high councils take place there and serious decisions are taken, and, in any case, whoever participates in the seventh astral level has reached the highest point of human evolution and strives, or more precisely, deserves to become a Master who has been put to the test in a way.

Some, but not many, reach the seventh astral level. They are few. However, there is no shortage. There is a large number, but not the multitude one finds on the seventh or sixth level, from the third, second and first level. There, one finds the presence of many discarnate as well as incarnate souls that wander into these well-known astral locations that their personal evolution allows them to during their physical sleep.

On the third level, there is a large congregation of people, as there is on the fourth level, where the crowd starts to grow sparser. On the fifth level, this sparsity is more evident. On the sixth level, the crowd is even sparser and on the seventh there is a large sparsity of souls; their numbers there are greatly limited.

The train route up is steep and rugged and it makes the train labour up slowly, decreasing speed and losing thrust as it ascends, because the journey demands real detachment from matter, as well as real internalization and/or spiritualization of the soul.

In our physical world, people who have activated or inherited clairvoyant ability from their previous lives appear once in a while. There are, however, very many categories of clairvoyants.

A person who receives the "gift" of clairvoyance doesn't immediately see the souls and their courses through the invisible worlds of the etheric and the astral world. This is rare.

Most of those with clairvoyant ability don't have these qualities. Usually, they see behind or through physical matter, they see the interior of matter, they see how the juices of the plants and the animals circulate within them and what work they do, they see the internal circulation of the organisms of other people, and the function of their organs. They also see immense distances through physical matter. They can see right through the earth. Still, people with clairvoyant ability can expand this ability they have to the whole physical-material universe.

From a spiritual point of view, this gift, though rare, is **not** considered to be of great importance. There are beings, spiritual Masters and Mystics, who may possess this ability to the fullest yet consider it to be very trivial and unworthy of mention and attention. Because their attention and interest is focused on the Monumental, on the Supreme, on the Matrixes-Ideas of the Father (Akashic Records – 8th Dimension, Spiritual and

Hyper-universes), on the Divine Masterpieces and on the Divine Being from which EVERYTHING derives.

From time to time, there are those with clairvoyant ability who can ascend the first step of the etheric material dimension adjacent to ours and observe what is happening there. That is to say, they see the descending or ascending souls, incarnate or discarnate; they see the life of these areas, the souls bound to earth, imprisoned of their own free will, after their physical death; on the etheric side of our world, they see the phenomenon of death unravelling itself in real time before their eyes, as they observe people passing away; they see the native beings whose permanent residence is the etheric world, as ours is the physical world.

Usually, clairvoyants on this level – if they have not randomly or accidentally discovered that they have this gift – become teachers for the rest of humanity despite themselves. It is rare for this far-sight to reach the upper layers of the etheric world. In fact, those who acquire this ability also gain their esoteric identity and self-recognition. They have the ability to see their previous lives and to assume, more consciously than any other person, their role before Creation, their soul, God and, of course, their fellowmen.

They are the ones who are appointed Masters of their fellowmen who cannot and are not entitled to have direct personal knowledge of the above, because their karma (that is, the burden they bear) forbids it and because they must function naturally and without prejudice in every one of their new incarnations, in relation with their fellowmen with whom they associated in previous lives and with whom, for karmic reasons, they must associate again in the present life, in order to settle the relationship and the obligations between them, without being affected by previous situations, positive or mainly negative, that they shared and for which they are called upon to find an equilibrium.

They must advance their evolution very much in order to approach similar experiences and to see and hear for themselves a greater or smaller part of the hidden Truth that governs, sets in motion and directs everything in our world. Otherwise, they **cannot** fathom the workings of these inextricably linked relationships of the souls that rule this incarnate (and discarnate) life of ours within the context of many consecutive incarnations, at times negative and at others positive or alternately, and they trigger a plethora of issues in need of a solution concerning old karmic debts created among us.

There is, however, one more category of superior beings in Creation that we call **Mystics.** They can do everything. They have Clairaudient and Clairvoyant abilities, Intuition, Knowledge of the individual soul, of the individual spirit, of Creation, and communion with the Divine Reality. **ONLY THEY. Nobody else.**

Everything emanates from the Free Will of every incarnated man-soul. With the free choices and deeds that every soul forms in thought, word and deed, it creates good or bad obligations that it will definitely be called upon to restore to their initial position. This is called Karma in Sanskrit.

Karma is the Law of Retributive Justice, the very history of our lives through which we present our current character and personality. And all this is the result of **our Free Choice** in **thought, word** and **deed** in our interaction with the physical-etheric matter-world and the other incarnated spirit-souls.

Every one of our thoughts, whether good or bad, creates a corresponding result, not only in the physical world but also in the etheric one. That's why we say that **karma is initially our thoughts and then our deeds.** Because with our deeds we directly or indirectly affect our surroundings, but with our thoughts we affect the whole universe-world either in a good or bad way.

Depending on all the deeds and days that we have formed in our life, we create the suitable vibrations, we collect the corresponding astral matter and in this way we construct the astral vessel, carrier, body in which we will end up as souls after our physical death.

All our thoughts and **all** our **deeds** are inscribed on this astral body and are waiting there to be handed over to us in full. Both the good as well as the bad. That's why the structure of the astral body differs in the density or sparsity of the molecules that make up its matter. Sometimes it is harder, thicker and heavier and at other times it is softer, thinner. The more refined and moral and superior a person's thinking becomes, the more refined this structure becomes.

A person is truly fortunate if he encounters a **true Master** on his path, a being who will explain the ways of esotericism and the meaning of life and one's duty towards it. **Absolutely no other value is greater than this.** As a matter of fact, if he finds himself at the feet of a **Mystic**, then a new age is born to this person. The age of integrated truth. This is a great matter, though rare.

The mortal and still karma-bearing person savours simple morsels of transcendental truths directly from the mouth of these Mystics or great spiritual Masters. What's more, he can converse with these beings and pose question upon question, ask for more and more clarifications and elucidations on the entire revealed range of exoteric, esoteric and spiritual truths.

And as you may realize, after all this, there is no better person to faithfully and capably serve – with everybody against them – the **UNIQUE TRUTHS OF THE MYSTICS** than the **actual student of such Divine Beings** who were granted, perhaps through divine providence or perhaps because they deserved it, the right to drink as deeply as possible directly from the Divine Substance which flows **from the mouth of these Greatest Beings of Creation.**

And, if we cannot hear these great and fully experienced truths directly from the mouth or the pen of the Mystics, we can learn about them from their immediate students, perhaps with lower vibrations but NEVER altered and NEVER made to comply with the human karma-bearing needs and the covert earthly or etheric wishes. Nor will they hear about combined forms of para-metaphysics or infantile versions of metaphysics usually promoted by imperfectly evolved people, within karma, and/or esoteric views combined with human inventions whose purpose it is to please the ego, to fulfil the need to impose oneself on others or even to make a profit, as in the case of commercial trusts that simply want to "sell" easily digestible "metaphysical knowledge", compatible with the earthly and not the real and accepted esoteric and spiritual needs of evolution and truth.

Now, just because one of our fellowmen has evolved or attained a certain degree of evolution, it doesn't mean he is a perfect being simply because, for example, he reached the sixth astral level. We've already mentioned that on the sixth astral level, people enjoy such calmness, such peace and such absolute beauty that they believe they have arrived at Paradise. And they form a conception that they have reached the end or that they have made a great spiritual conquest or ascended the highest peak. Metaphorically speaking, they put a full stop.

Therefore, they also put an end to their evolution and at the same time, they idealize and equate it with perfection. Which is completely untrue. In a nutshell, they don't want to hear and they don't accept the existence of superior truths and the continuation of evolution. They are content and satisfied with what they have learnt (besides, the same thing happens on the lower astral steps) and they don't listen to the Guides-Masters of the dimension in which they are in (doesn't the same also happen on earth with a large number of incarnated souls not even listening to what the incarnated spiritual Masters or Mystics say and write?), and as a result, they remain, at their own peril, at the same point of evolution, without advancing further as they should.

So, they induce other new-comers to do the same – which is not necessarily bad –, but by insisting that this is the end, that this is everything, you close the door on evolution. Do you understand now what we mean? There are stages. There are different phases of evolution. There is a phase that brings one's first accomplishment and unrivalled peace and beauty to the soul. But that doesn't mean that one has reached the end. **For real evolution starts timidly and never ends.**

For instance, someone who "meditates", who practices advanced Hypnotism – Self-hypnotism – Mediumship and **not** high-level Meditation or Mysticism (the real experience of meditation essentially begins from the 1st mental step and upwards and its highest level is by the Father's side), may find himself at some point on the sixth astral level and get a taste of this beauty.

If he doesn't have a Master who can correct his mistakes, or if he does put pays no attention to his advice and counsel, or if he simply satisfies and builds his ego when he finds himself in this situation, he will very likely come back "running" and will say "this way people, the truth is here and I'm ... its representative". Do you see what's happening? If the people involved in hypnotism are not properly trained and well-read in the Truths of the Mystics, they make tragic errors or, as they say in common parlance, they make "howlers".

People make 'howlers' in esoteric matters as well, some involuntarily.

That's the reality governing human needs. It also governs these matters, which are weighty and profound; they are not simple. Don't be fooled by the fact that we joke about them and mention them in passing. What usually happens is that we are dazzled by the words of such men and we focus our interest only on them without consulting the Mystics and their testimonies, which are difficult to comprehend and require effort to do so. Or to put it more bluntly, for those of us who know a thing or two, we see them, we hear them and we smile to ourselves or become frustrated at the deception people so "voluntarily" fall victim to.

However, all these situations, whether big or small, hide immense meanings of Truths, Esoteric Truths. And a stratification of things. Which are not easily grasped. You must have a Mystic to unwind them for you at whatever cost and labour. You must have moral stature, a healthy mind, an old and experienced Soul. A karmic unburdening. You must have the moral order of things within you – to serve it. To fight for what's best. To improve your evolution. To improve your environment. To improve society, even with your thoughts. And with your daily routine. Because that is where you can and must function.

And all this has a more general impact as much on society–the world as on you personally who are evolving and cultivating your vibration, your way of thinking; and as a result, you go up a step, ascending from the one you belong to at the moment. You may belong to the third. You may belong to the fourth. Of course, this holds true for those who approach esoteric knowledge with genuine interest and not with feigned, artificial interest or simply out of curiosity or snobbism. Not when they have to be carried to acquire the knowledge. Not when they have to be forced to acquire the knowledge. Only when they come of their own accord out of genuine personal interest and because they have a facility for it. When they have a flair for it. An inclination. A tendency. Those who are attracted to esotericism and attend various training and educational functions belong to the fourth astral level and higher.

But for some exceptions, no one can be taught the esoteric Truth if they have not already ascended to the fourth astral level, the reason being that they cannot handle it and they are not really interested in the Truth. They are only interested in their exoteric ego and the acquisitive aspect of things. Nothing else. They don't care a snap. Is there a Father or is there not a

Father? Is there Creation or is there not Creation? Is there a God or is there not a God? Are there or aren't there Mystics? Is there or isn't there Superior Knowledge? Is there or isn't there a Moral Order? All mine. Do you understand?

That's why the Masters accept students from the fourth astral level. The students are not accomplished beings. They are people who have much to learn, and whoever of them realizes and desires to do so benefits from it. Those who don't wish to learn can stay where they are. Very simple. There is no pressure or coercion to ascend nor are concessions made at the expense of and against the other children of the Lord. But the knowledge is present now and they are burdened by it. And when you are burdened by the Knowledge, the Divine Knowledge, any mistake you make is made bigger. And bears more karmic weight. Because you cannot say that you didn't know, you didn't hear, you didn't see. These things must be said. But, at the same time, you have the unparalleled opportunities and unique possibilities for esoteric development that you never had before. Given, of course, that you wish to take advantage of them in your exoteric and esoteric life.

In the passage above, I briefly described what the post-mortem order of things is so that you can have a basic-substantial idea and so that you can detect what is happening within you as well as around you concerning this matter. Already from the fourth etheric level, the soul knows where it will go. And in most cases the soul starts to weep and express an unwillingness, a refusal, a fear for what it knows will happen.

In this way, it is carried away by a type of electromagnetic breath – energy that takes it where it deserves to be. Why? Because it is on the fourth etheric step that borders with the first astral level that we find the beings of the diaconate, the etheric police officers (Devas), who arrest the souls when they enter these areas of the fourth etheric level and unblock their memory.

As soon as their memory is unblocked, they retrieve consciousness of the previous incarnations and karmas they had undergone and not undergone. That is, they acknowledge their entire course as souls and as reincarnations.

Automatically, they become cognizant of the real deeds and the days they have formed as well as where they are destined to go according to the level of evolution they now fully acknowledge as having, with all they have done and all they have not done. And where exactly will they go? In other words, where will they end up on the astral level. Will they stop on the first, on the second, on the third? Those that are to stop somewhere on the first three steps make things difficult or refuse to advance. They don't want to. However, their course is predestined and obligatory now.

The souls that don't wish to advance from the three lower etheric steps to the fourth superior etheric step choose, like other escapees (souls kept captive on earth), to stay where there is no police and where the

Creator has made an asylum of freedom for these souls until they grow bored or decide that the moment has come for them to move on, or to allow themselves to be arrested by the etheric police (devas), or that a master or another more mature soul crosses their path and explains their position to them and the obligations they have towards their evolution.

There they stir up and relive, in an etheric state, the experiences, memories and desires they had from the period of their physical life as if they were experiencing them normally, with the only difference being that there are no physical organs and tools of the material body to ground all these acts that in essence are imitations of what they had lived, and reproductions or tendencies to revisit places they had frequented as physical presences in our material world, but now visit in their etheric clothing-body and without the ability to communicate with the physical people.

These souls move between the first, second and third etheric step, retaining their etheric body, although they should have dissolved it and departed for the astral world where their evolution calls them, but because they wish to "savour" their old earthly experiences and adventures that satisfy them, they remain behind, like high-school dropouts, failing to experience the continuation of their evolutionary course.

All incarnated souls pass through the etheric level in order to reach the astral sub-level/sub-dimension that their level of evolution guides them to. Many souls leave immediately without stopping at all in the etheric world. But for some reason, other souls voluntarily anchor themselves in the etheric world and remain entangled there, halting their evolution. With time, of course, they too ascend but with greater difficulty than if they had left directly or within the expected time frames, which are the first three days, nine days or forty days after their physical death.

If one of these souls strays from the three first etheric steps onto the fourth etheric sub-level/sub-dimension or is simply picked up by a patrolling Deva, it is arrested by this angelic being and is brought to the appropriate etheric police station, where its memory is unblocked. It will see what it really is, it will recognize its deeds and its days and it will see where it is to go.

Some of these souls sing hymns and rejoice as soon as they recognize what they are and where they are destined to go because of the high position they hold, which corresponds to them because of the history of their physical life.

And it's quite natural that some of them are not at all pleased with the continuation of their course. But that is to be expected, given the course they had taken. What can we do? Justice is justice. And it is **Divine Justice,** because it doesn't make distinctions or exceptions, but is administered justly for every soul. We can't take advantage of contacts, friends, relatives, money, status, privilege here. There's no saying, "Come on, he's a good guy," when someone has butchered and exploited 15 of his fellowmen. Everyone is equal here **WHATEVER one was** during one's physical life.

Here, absolute justice is served and a Divine Order is observed; an order that does not resemble the human type, because it examines a person **IN-DEPTH** by looking at their deeds and days and not their superficial image or clothing-coverings or their transient incarnations; it is an in-depth look at a person's many incarnations with more attention being paid to the most recent one.

As soon as the discarnate soul receives its memory and it ascertains its real position in evolution, it appears directly before the **Karmic Committee** of the **Three plus One Masters of Karma**, which is appointed by the **White Celestial or Spiritual Hierarchy of the 33** whose role it is to ensure the actualization of the **Divine Plan**.

The **Karmic Committee** has full jurisdiction in the 13th physical-etheric dimension, the 12th astral dimension and the 11th lower-mental dimension. The committee and the same just spirit-souls have been trying souls from the onset of postdiluvian times until today.

It is a four-member committee, with its fourth member acting as a substitute and usually absent due to missions it has been sent on. According to Greek Mythology, these individuals are **Minos, Rhadamanthus** and **Aeacus**, while **Sarpedon** is the one who is usually absent. In Christian terminology, they are the **four Archangels**. In Hindu tradition, it is **Maharajan**.

The Karmic Committee constitutes the executive body of the Law of Retributive Justice (Karma) and is located in a special area of the second sub-level/sub-dimension of the astral world.

When the soul stands trial before the Committee, there are also two witnesses present. One is the angel-deva accompanying it and the other is an earthly discarnate friend or relative of the soul's own choosing or a random bystander of terrible crimes the soul has committed in order to emphasize the intellectual state at the moment of the crime.

The alternating president of the Committee always makes the final decision (two votes) while all the others have one vote each.

With the unsealing of its memory on the 4th etheric step, the soul reads its karmic note and it becomes fully cognizant of its position. Next, it puts on the astral body with which it will be brought before the Karmic Criterion of the Three plus One Masters of Karma through a special walkway of neutral vibrations that serves the ascension and the descent of the spirit-souls.

Before the Committee, it will see its entire life in all its detail on a special dial. Then the verdict of the Karmic Committee follows. It decides how many years the discarnate will have to remain at a sub-level of the astral world for the re-examination of its deeds, before it is given the opportunity for a new incarnation in the physical world.

The decision is usually unanimous and states the

place/sub-dimension where the soul will be sent in order to fulfil its work – sentence and the duration of its stay until it acknowledges its errors, repents for them and properly prepares itself for a new incarnation, carrying with it a part of the general karma it has accumulated in the course of thousands of years through its very many incarnations.

How long the souls dwell on the astral sub-dimensions may vary, in terms of earthly perception of time, from some hundreds of years to thousands of years.

Then, as soon as the discarnate soul is deemed ready for descent – in consultation with the karmic committee – it is always accompanied by an **etheric note** which discloses how it will spend its life in our physical world.

In this note, both the time of birth as well as the time of death are determined to an unbelievable degree of accuracy, as are many personal, family, social events that will take place during its incarnation.

All the bodily diseases as well as every bitterness and joy that the formed soul will experience are recorded. Restrictions have been set everywhere and they are quite tight. All the obligations that the soul must fulfil have been analytically set out.

The obligations taken on during previous incarnations of the soul are only a part of our old debts. The plan or program has been formed wisely and with divine justice.

So, it has been estimated how many things our

man-soul can bear, pay off and endure in the current incarnation.

Many people ask what happens with those who commit suicide. According to esoteric tradition, those who commit suicide – that is, who voluntarily end their life – quickly return in order to be reincarnated. They appear before the karmic committee, after they have unsealed their memory. They are made to see the tragic mistake they have made and they are obliged, as a rule, to be reincarnated in order to make arrangements for its destination from exactly the same point it was suddenly interrupted, by right of the free will they possess and with which they terminated it before it was completed – again according to the plan they had set of their own free will before this incarnation.

They make a serious karmic mistake because they attempt to run away from the problems and the situations of their life that correspond to them by right of their karma, without taking into account that there is no way they can escape from their obligations, whatever they may be.

In fact, the Christian church denies funeral rites and prayers for those who commit suicide.

We, however, will respond with philosophy as a guide, and specifically the Esoteric-Metaphysical Philosophy of the Mystics, which considers suicide to be a very grave error on behalf of the person, in that they had a life before them and they threw it away.

Why?

Because they had problems, because they didn't see a way out, because they didn't see a light at the end of the tunnel. But what they threw away was something they had to go through and they neglected to do so or were too cowardly to handle it. They lacked the endurance and strength to fulfil the duty they had willingly assumed before they had even been incarnated in our world. On coming here, they displayed pusillanimity and timidity in face of the life difficulties that act as their karmic counterbalance.

That's why, according to Metaphysics, as a soul, everyone is obliged to pay for what corresponds to him. However, in the case of suicide, a person adds a particularly heavy karma to the load on their back, one they didn't have in the past.

And how could it be otherwise, when each of us is here for a purpose and a reason and somebody renounces this reason because of a moment of inability, a dark moment or a kind of depression or for some other reason and chooses to commit the desperate act of suicide?

Isn't this cowardice in face of life? Isn't it cowardice in face of duty? Shouldn't the soul be made to understand this? How? When it ascends, regains its memory and stands before the Karmic Committee, it will acquire full knowledge of its error and it will clearly see its deeds and its days. It will go through an intensive school course and immediately thereafter, it will descend in order to resume exactly where it had violently and unexpectedly stopped its incarnation – only now with the additional burden of the new karmic error. There is no interruption in evolution. There are simply temporary stops or delays tied to the free will of a person.

Do you think that all the incarnated beings here evolve normally? No. They too do not evolve normally and according to the mutually agreed upon Plan; with the different events of their life, they simply pay for their old karmas. Most people, however, go against the Divine Plan for the advance of their evolution. And they move forward at a snail's pace.

But the choice of suicide directly weakens their position. In fact, by leaving, they don't remain on the three first etheric steps but go directly to the fourth etheric level, where the Devas welcome them and make arrangements for their progress. And this occurs because they don't have strong bonds behind them on earth to hang on to, or perhaps, they don't want to have; they are disappointed by everyone and everything, though they shouldn't be. And they leave directly, without wasting time.

Whereas most of the others who leave physically have something to keep them behind. They have relatives. They have friends. They have loved ones. They have material acquisitions. They have the flowers and nature. They have their house, material goods. They have their bank accounts and desires to fulfil. They have different interests and strong passions. To each his own.

So they have many interests behind, many reasons to stay and quench their curiosity, many reasons to return and see what is happening or to relive moments of their physical life, recreating them through etheric reality or visiting places and areas where they enjoyed living in order to recall and to directly experience the satisfaction of past events and relations.

But, by doing so, they don't go on to the Light and the Etheric Tunnel that opens before them to lead them to the superior single dimensions of the Lord that they themselves have prepared to receive them.

If the valve of life (Sutratma) isn't turned off, a person doesn't die. First, the soul must command that the valve on the crown of a person's head that lets in the Essence of Life be turned off before the phenomenon of death appears in the physical body.

The dissolution of the etheric body is the natural next step of physical death. With the physical death, the etheric body stands above the physical body, trying to supply it with life and to revive it, to awaken it. In other words, the etheric body – along with the immature, unripe and dazed soul – stand behind the physical body and try to bring it back to life.

Ninety-nine per cent of the times, it cannot revive it. The valve of Sutratma has closed and it doesn't open again. There is a one per cent chance it will manage to re-open the valve of life or activate the etheric mechanisms of some chakras that still contain stored energy, and then we say that we have the **death trance** or, more rarely, **vampirism**. These are two completely different phenomena. They need special analysis in order to explain how and why they occur and under what conditions. In order to explain the nature of these phenomena and other relevant matters, a new informative book is already underway.

Many souls who depart this world through death don't cease retaining their memories and the strong bonds with their loved ones and their beloved places or objects or passions. When these bonds, these people that love them beckon them with constant and strong thoughts of loss, with thoughts of concern, with thoughts of love and a need for reunion, they create a hold on the souls that are departing and they don't allow them to move freely towards their destination.

They retain the interest of the souls and don't allow them to orientate themselves in relation with their needs and in the direction of their evolution, which imposes their physical separation from their loved ones in the physical dimension they are leaving behind them.

The souls have every reason to be drawn to those left behind and to wish to be psychically or etherically connected with them, especially when their desires and bonds with the physical world are still very strong.

That's why Esotericism advises people not to constantly call back the departed with their thoughts. That's also the reason why the third day, the ninth day and the fortieth day of the mourning period and the annual memorial services are so significant in religion.

It's also a way to remind the departed souls that their destination is no longer the physical world and that they are dead in this world and they must now – as souls – go to the destination that corresponds to the evolution of their soul. That they must move forward. That they must not remain in the intermediate etheric world that is a transit area, a passageway, and not a suitable dwelling place for them.

Some wonder whether it is the fear of the... unknown or more precisely the fear of the trial of the souls for their deeds and days by the Karmic Committee that retains them in the intermediate etheric world?

From what is known in Esotericism, this happens, as a rule, to those souls that have esoteric knowledge about the phenomenon of death. And usually those that know are of two qualities, of two categories.

The first category of souls concerns the savants, the initiated and the Masters, who don't have anything to fear from death since they have toiled with self-sacrifice, selflessly and with love for the good of their own evolution and of society, always according to their powers. This is especially true for the Masters who had crossed the threshold of death while they were still alive and who had moved consciously from the nether to the higher worlds.

Therefore, particularly for them, this is a natural and absolutely normal procedure, the only difference being that the cord connecting them to the specific etheric-physical body that served the needs of this particular soul's incarnation in our physical world is now definitively severed.

The second large category is the evil-doing primitive souls that have many reasons to feel disquiet and fear for their deeds and days on earth. And just as the evildoers know much when they are physical matter, they sense or instinctively or subconsciously suspect that their situation is precarious in the etheric reality. As cunning beings, they are generally more advanced than the average human soul in the understanding of things that concern them.

As we have already mentioned above, the malevolent souls correspond evolutionally to the first and to the second astral step/sub-dimension. Some of them attempt to create vampire-like and other phenomena in order to return to the physical body as "living" beings (the more accurate expression would be as "living dead").

They try to do so using sorcery and various other means they may have in mind or that they persistently experiment with, given their cunning nature. These are things of which esotericism knows the cause and know-how. In any case, they fight tooth and nail to succeed in their endeavour.

Once in a great while, they may do so. Certainly, this doesn't mean that their wish is actualized. We have many historical, documented examples proving that these phenomena have occurred in the past, perhaps even in our days, though this is more difficult since, apart from the coffin and the soil, a marble monument is placed over the grave.

Clearly, the above may occur only when we bury the body of the dead, because when a body is cremated and we bury the ashes of the dead, then there is no hope of these pathogenic phenomena occurring, as the physical body has totally ceased existing, and it cannot be reconstituted, unless a superior being/mystic intervenes, and this only under extraordinary conditions due to the special nature of a mission, using ectoplasmic materializations as a method, and not by incompetent and low spiritual evolutions that know, act on behalf of and consciously serve only evil.

But all these phenomena are very rare and are not always related to vampirism, especially as it is portrayed in most television series these days. It is presented in a very imaginary and silly manner, lacking any truth, and totally distorting the reality which metaphysics accepts and uses to explain these phenomena.

Because we believe a sound esoteric, scientific briefing is much needed; one that follows the esoteric tradition, free of human inventiveness, imagination and, of course, commercial benefits, we hope, in the near future, to publish a special book about death trances, vampirism, ghosts and fairies (parallel evolutions), so that apart from all this imaginary and essentially commercial trivia – so abundant in our days and, in many cases, falsely documented – one who is truly interested can find the corresponding authentic view of the Mystics so as to comprehend and compare these phenomena – without being trapped or wishing to remain trapped in a false and non-existent second virtual reality beyond what one is already experiencing in the world of matter and which one considers dominant, though it too is fake and clearly of an educational nature and indispensable for evolution.

Here we face another great issue on which metaphysics has a clear position and view. In metaphysics, there are many reasons why it is believed that cremation is preferable for the dead than the slow decomposition process of the body. Apart from the reasons of external hygiene, there are also esoteric reasons.

As long as the body remains intact, it starts with a slow process of decay or decomposition, but because the etheric body in which the soul is now lodged has a particular love for its mate, the physical body, it cannot part with it so easily or automatically.

It is not only a matter of nostalgia, but there is also a need for the etheric body to reconnect with the physical body. And the etheric body makes every effort, by virtue of its nature and position of power, to revive the physical body. However, it rarely succeeds in doing so. But it tries. This, however, is unbearable for the soul that must leave but cannot do so if the etheric body has not dissolved. The etheric body must dissolve in order for the soul to leave. And so, the soul remains trapped in the etheric body.

One way to accelerate the destruction of the etheric

body, or otherwise the energy body, is to cremate the physical body. Because, as soon as the physical body is cremated, the etheric body finds no point of reference or connection to unite with and reconnect its love. Because it is the negative-positive poles that have learned to polarize.

And so the etheric body begins to waste away and dissolve, to self-destruct due to the absence of the physical body. Not because the physical body was destroyed but because the etheric body no longer has an entity to call on and try to restore and commune with.

Therefore, in this sense, metaphysics holds this view and position. And it maintains that the cremation of the dead is preferable because, in this way, the prisoners of Earth, the captive spirits of Earth (spirit-souls) decrease in number and it allows for the rapid departure and restoration to their corresponding degree of evolution.

The opposing view is that this must not take place because our bodies will be resurrected on... the Second Coming. But this is a very childish perception of the limits, the rights and the potential of the soul, of the spirit and of God himself. It is too infantile.

He built a whole Creation, and we're wondering if a body will be dissolved and if it will rise again/be resurrected in order that... the soul be judged? At any given moment, a Mystic (let alone the Creator-God who created everything from Zero) or a high standing Spiritual Master is considered to be in full control of matter

– since they are above matter – and in a position to recompose, at will or as needed, the material body to its entirety; though He rarely does so and only in order to fulfil a special duty, and not to satisfy the material needs of the other enslaved souls that are dependent on matter, whatever opposing dogmatic approaches maintain.

The final judgement of the souls doesn't necessarily require a material body (and even if the soul is incarnated in matter, it is destroyed at the End of Time or the End of the World or the Second Advent) and it starts from where the perception of existence is more universal, from the etheric-astral-mental world and upwards and at whichever higher dimension every soul finds itself ascending evolutionarily. We explain all of this more analytically in our other works (*The Apocalypse of John as Explained by Master Nikolaos A. Margioris*).

The soul that is released from matter and karma lies above matter and controls it. It has no reason to wear matter again in order to be assessed by the Creator in a material creation that collapses by order of the Creator.

Behind the belief that material attire is needed for the souls before judgement, we find hidden the strong adherence of people (whatever status they hold) to the external carrier, to the external tangible distinctive feature of one's fellowmen and a detachment from the esoteric truth and the spiritualization-perfectionism that is the true destination and occurs by means of psycho-spiritual actualization – perfection from the 8th, 7th and especially from the 6th Spiritual Dimension and upwards, inwards, within the very domain of the Creator, where his Hyper-universes exist.

People's attachment to matter is such that even after their physical death, the transitional procedures of the soul from the etheric to the astral are hindered or even postponed indefinitely in some cases and form the earthbound souls, the ghosts and many more tortured and unhappy beings of this nature.

And this is solely due to the attachment of the etheric carrier, which could either be identical to the physical carrier or quite different, to matter and to the immaturity and ignorance of the souls concerning the beyond, the afterlife and the true destination of their evolution.

The well-trained etheric bodies self-dissolve within three days. Those that are lesser trained and less informed last nine days and the untrained and primitive etheric beings need forty days after the death of the physical body to dissolve.

Of course, there are those that do not dissolve and constitute a pathogenic society of souls, called earthbound souls or prisoners of earth, that are kept of their own free will at this intermediary stage of our etheric world, especially the three etheric steps, for long intervals of time.

The memorial services that take place act as reminders to the departing souls that they don't belong to the world of the living anymore, that they belong on the other side, with the other community, that of the discarnate souls, and that they must move on in order to take on their new position and their new duties.

What relatives and friends who remain behind need to do is make sure that the thoughts they convey are positive, encouraging, calming and educational, urging them to continue and move on to their now discarnate evolution without any inhibitions or delays.

But that's why more experience and deeper esoteric knowledge are required. And naturally, one needs a clear head, which those who have lost a loved one usually don't have. Because at that moment things become bad, heavy, clouded and come to a standstill. Everything is gone. There are no more theories, metaphysics, histories, documents; everything collapses under the weight of the "loss", of the physical loss of our loved one.

Why? Because we haven't been schooled, as have children of other cultures, to cry at the birth of the newly incarnated souls – for the burdens and pains they will endure during their earthly passage – and celebrate and rejoice at their death because the soul has rid itself of the constraining bodily-material limitations and has found a greater and higher freedom. It is a temporary deliverance of the soul from the compulsory bonds, from the untold hardships of a physical body.

So, when we lose a loved one, we have to realize – as hard and difficult as it may be at first – that the time has come for this person to leave. This is not our permanent abode, to remain here forever, nor are we eternal. We are transient beings.

We have to understand this. And it is also like a test, a type of training in the attachment that is created between people and the possessiveness that accompanies it.

It is a form of training we undergo in order not to become attached. As much for the one who departs as for the one who stays behind. For the ones who depart because they must go on their way, so they must disconnect themselves from this world and move on to the next. But at the same time, they must also disconnect from all the animate and three-dimensional material relations they had with their fellow beings.

And for those who remain behind, they have to adapt to this reality, to cope with it in as balanced and responsible a way as possible, to remain true to the metaphysical truth – for those who have discovered it – , to take initiative, and to take their own independent steps, no longer dependent on the physical presence – help – support – favour of others.

Those who have no metaphysical education may have gained religious instruction-guidance (or at any rate common sense). Because we have been given religion and it is helpful. It is a balm for many people. But because there is a lack of knowledge and experience, when one comes face to face with what religion narrates so simply, or metaphysics more analytically and extensively, there is disbelief, faithlessness, moroseness, pain and adversity.

There is doubt. There is always incertitude at the back – and even in the front – of one's mind about this reality. And if all these things don't exist, what then? What could happen, we ask. Whatever the case, our need to have our loved ones eternally near us is futile. Because we do not remain here eternally either. From some point on, it is a matter of experience, knowledge and seniority of the soul.

The candle we light at funerals symbolizes the person's soul and we light it in memory of the deceased. It is the memory of this person as a soul that we honour, and it is the evolution of this soul we are concerned about.

For we must know that the spiritual link is not destroyed by virtue of the physical absence of the body of the person who once lived and is now deceased, whose soul departed from the earthly world.

The nexus of relationships formed among the people remains imperishable and accompanies the souls in the afterlife as well as in their next life and their reincarnation.

These are called karmic bonds, karmic relationships that connect the souls with each other. Therefore, nothing is lost. What happens is that we temporarily lose – for a few years – the direct, live three-dimensional conscious relationship we had with the deceased.

If we had some clairvoyant ability or conscious

out-of-body experience we would see the soul of our beloved emerging before us in its etheric or astral clothing and we would be able to converse with it and discuss any issues we had.

In many cases, this happens to the average person unconsciously, during moments of deep contemplation and particularly during moments of sleep when the soul leaves the body and moves around in the etheric and astral regions, meeting many of the friends and acquaintances it was connected with and is given the opportunity to commune with them again.

However, these wanderings of the soul during sleep are not fully realized by consciousness because during those moments the subconscious prevails. Many of these meetings, whether agreeable or disagreeable, remain as faint or clear dreams to remind us that within everything that exists and everything that happens, the relationships of the souls are not severed but remain intact, with or without a physical body. It is estimated that 30% - 40% of our dreams are meetings of this type, with immaterial or discarnate beings, earthly or not, but also with incarnate acquaintances or relatives or friends with whom we meet either in the etheric or in the astral world during the wanderings in the sky we all indulge in during natural sleep.

Perhaps we will have the opportunity to discuss the world of dreams more thoroughly in one of our future books.

Here we must mention the great contribution of

spiritualism to the contact and the two-way communication between the incarnate and the discarnate. The whole subject of Spiritualism constitutes a separate scientific branch of Esotericism which, together with the branch of Hypnotism-Orthopsychism, otherwise known as ancient Greek hypnotherapy, can aid in the study of post-mortem problems, always under strict conditions and with the guidance of a medium and a properly trained participating team to organize controlled and safe spiritual experiments concerning contact with the invisible and mainly with superior discarnate beings that can convey esoteric knowledge on a whole range of metaphysical issues, and to also conduct the rare and superior experiments of spiritualism concerning the materializations of superior entities for consultation, teaching and for actual three-dimensional confirmation for those present of the existence of the invisible and the post-mortem continuation of the soul.

In fact, such experiments have been conducted at various times and in various places on earth in the past, with varying degrees of success, and for reasons that are not very clear nowadays, they have been almost entirely abandoned and not much is said about them now. Perhaps the reason for this was a lack of serious researchers as well as a lack of suitable intermediating ectoplasm. The existing mediums, apart from those on the... market, only communicate with the invisible or with ... extra-terrestrials and don't possess any ectoplasmic exudations for the manifestation of these superior phenomena of materialization, and the experts – guides of such mediumships have actually ceased to exist. Possibly because the burden of a new technocratic materialism combined with all the above hinders the conduct of more serious, more qualitative and... more difficult experiments of this type and level.

In fact, the greatest and best-known experiments of materialization were conducted in the past by the great English chemist and physicist Sir William Crookes, discoverer of the unknown element Thallium and inventor of many other patents.

He had the good fortune to find a young ectoplasmic medium, Florence Cook, with whom, over a period of three years, he conducted profound and complete experiments in materialization in the presence of many scientists who signed the minutes before and after the execution of these rare experiments.

In these experiments, the Hindu princess, Katie King, gradually materialized from the exuded ectoplasm of the medium, going through all thirteen (13) stages of a complete morphic-physical materialisation of an invisible, etheric and discarnate being-soul, which manifested itself in physical form in order to teach and answer a variety of questions of the experimenters who were present.

These experiments were conducted over a period of three years and produced exceptional and rare information on the whole subject. This information must be retrieved once more and should be updated and used by all esotericists in their fight against materialism. These vital documents of the clear and miraculous findings must be disseminated in every direction.

We consider it of the utmost importance to seek and train mediums and experimenters of such calibre so as to arrive at a sound esoteric scientific basis that could utilise all the true and authentic means and methods of spiritualism in order that both modern man and the scientific community be presented with the confirmation-proof needed for them to closely cooperate with esotericists.

To this purpose, our first priority is to write an introductory book on Scientific Spiritualism and its various applications, and then another one on Hypnotism-Orthopsychism, and later to translate into English the only relevant, well-documented and profound works from the immense experience of Nikolaos Margioris.

In closing, it is useful to add that besides the above, the greatest gift a person can receive is the **Esoteric Education of Mystics**, which they must learn and study in depth, and then apply to the fullest through the development of Meditation and Mysticism.

Meditation is the main means that every person has at their disposal to perceive and experience all the metaphysical problems, not to mention that it will assist them in becoming aware of their own psycho-spiritual status and the Divine.

Only through meditation – mysticism can a person

reach perfection/become spiritualized; everything else is of partial and marginal value and usefulness. We wholeheartedly wish that for everybody.

THE CAUSES OF DEATH

First of all, in a world where everything is composed of material elements that are combined in order that a morphic expression/presence be produced – always under the force and power of an individual spirit-soul (human) and/or of a collective soul (animals, plants, minerals, planets, solar systems, galaxies, etc.) – it is reasonable for this presence, which is a combination of material and temporary elements, to gradually deconstruct. Whatever is born, sooner or later, is led to the fatal end that is death.

Matter itself is a temporary crystallization – solidification of Energy (Prana) that holds this cohesion together thanks to the presence of the spirit-soul within it and the flow of the Life Force that is controlled by the spirit-soul. By its very nature and creation, matter has the tendency to physically waste away, to gradually decompose.

So, it is in the nature of matter to need revival at regular intervals. This revival gradually leads to the loosening of the joints of matter since the Essence of Life that is poured into matter throughout the years loses its initial drive and allows the human body to waste away, to let its functions fall into decline, and by tightly closing the valve of the etheric apparatus Sutratma, it leads to the death of the physical carrier.

So, apart from the revival of the physical carrier (and the matter that surrounds it) which occurs with death, the soul is given the opportunity to rid itself of the suffocating bonds of an obligatory incarnation and to settle karmic loose ends – some heavy, some light – as well as to offer the soul a temporary repose after the endless hardships it suffered during human life.

The basic cause of death is a person's Karma that accompanies all of us and determines how many years we will live, what karma-obligations and what experiences we will accumulate, and many other issues that concern our individual soul and personal evolution.

When the spirit gives the signal, the soul obeys and closes the valve that supplies Prana, thus allowing death to arrive and guide the soul out of the body, beside the etheric body, which will also be called upon to dissolve in order that the soul can ascend to the astral world – dimension, wearing the corresponding astral protective suit of the sub-dimension to which it belongs evolutionally.

There, it will start assimilating the experiences and the deeds it produced during this incarnation. Every incarnated soul, advancing evolutionally toward the esoteric, slightly refines the physical matter that surrounds it, within and without its body. In other words, what takes place is a refinement of physical matter, a slight increase in its vibrations, a fine-tuning, a mutation that occurs in three age periods.

Above all, why does death occur?

For regeneration to occur. For without death we have no regeneration. No regeneration of the soul's powers. No regeneration of the body's strength and drive, of its material constitution that accompanies and supports the incarnation of the soul that must occur. Why?

As people age, they lose interest and their desire to acquire knowledge, experiences and make dreams for the future declines. This means that there are age phases-stages that are related to the physical age and strength of people that bring them all the closer to the phenomenon of death.

These age milestones are initially the first three seven-year periods of a person's age ($3 \times 7 = 21$) when the drive and desire for life are very strong. During this time, a person is defined by large quantities of high-quality Prana. And that's why we see such vitality and activity among the young until the age of twenty-one.

The second stage of the $5 \times 7 = 35$ years concerns the five seven-year periods of life after the first twenty-one years. During this period, the frequency with which Prana enters the body gradually starts to decline and its inflow becomes all the more restricted. It decreases. Little by little. And as a result, a corresponding course follows, in which a person receives less and less energy and life force from prana as compared to the initial first age period.

Finally, a third age period follows which is that of the aged – while the previous one was the age of maturity, a sort of middle age – an old age when a person may reach up to one hundred and five years of age at least. This constitutes the other seven-year clusters, 7×7=49 years. Final total 21+ 35+49=105 years.

During this third period, the pranic flow has been greatly reduced, and that is why we see the body starting to waste away, wrinkles forming, and people's mobility, cognitive skills, and strength declining. Little by little, a person begins to deteriorate. The body starts being unable to regenerate with the speed and rapidity it used to, and so inherent problems of aging begin in the human organism. There is a decline in the body and the mind, in the brain that is, because it too is composed of matter. In other words, matter begins to disintegrate. Gradually, it starts losing its initial strength even more, because much fewer quantities of Prana flow in compared to the inflow it had during the first years of its incarnation.

The amount of prana decreases even more and at some point death crosses your path. So, regeneration is needed in order for somebody to regain matter with new force, with new power, with new life, with new pranic support to fulfil one's obligations and to produce the work one is required to.

Therefore, a revival is needed. The soul needs respite from the intrigues of matter and the karmic trials it suffers there. It also needs to assimilate everything it has formed or experienced during its life, with death being a transitional stage. The soul will go, will rethink and will fertilize everything it has produced during its life and it will come back to be incarnated, regenerated, strengthened and ... ready to fight. So, a temporary detachment from matter is required, and that is exactly what death is.

What's more, others need to come as well. Out with the old, in with the new. How will this happen? We have arrivals, a high turnout; we also have departures. Where will this situation lead to? World population has reached seven billion.

It is within physical matter-the physical world that the essence of a soul's evolution takes place; its reopening to the higher dimensions-worlds with the activation of the corresponding carriers of each region, their awakening.

In antediluvian times and civilizations, people's residence in matter lasted as long as Methuselah. It is estimated that mortals stayed on earth for one thousand years at those times. And that's why the human race fell into decay... because of boredom and an indifference towards physical life.

That's why our responsible invisible brothers determined that our stay on earth should not exceed one hundred years. The purpose of this restriction on the length of our stay on earth is to give the soul the opportunity to acquire a predetermined amount of experience. Beyond this fixed time limit, the soul longs for the return to the old, where it has left not only its memories but also its loved ones as well. Of course, little by little, these limits are gradually being exceeded once more.

WHAT IS DEATH?

Death is the interruption of human life or of human physical presence on our planet. What's more, it is the rejection of the physical-etheric body from the spirit-soul and its extrication from the nets of lower matter.

Furthermore, death is an imperative journey of the soul to the adjacent thymo-astral or thymo-astric dimension, the twelfth, where it will remain in the very area that our own soul has prepared in order to re-examine the earthly events, in which it lived, acted and actively participated.

Death is also the dissolution of the physical-etheric protective suit/body of the spirit-soul itself in order to construct another one, a new one for the continuation of life and the acquisition of a new kind of experience, which its old vessel didn't allow. In addition, death is the renewal of matter.

The matter that accommodates us has a basic and

permanent demand: that it be renewed. The renewal of matter occurs with psycho-spiritual intervention. In order to take shape, our spirit-soul gathers material molecules and elements and uses them to construct our physical body. Then our essence, the creative proto-energy (prana) is obliged to retain the natural elements, by watering them with ESSENCE in order that they become vitalized and converted into the familiar living-animate matter, and that beings become carriers of living matter instead of dead matter.

Death is the repose of the soul; after the soul has shaken off its heavier clothing or the armour it bears so as to enter superior worlds to the one of form. Consequently, man needs sleep/rest in order to detoxify and, in general, to regenerate his soul that is in charge not only during states of alertness/consciousness, but also during hypnosis – sleep – subconsciousness; it needs to rest and assimilate all that it acquired during its earthly life and manifestation.

And that's how old age arrives. The physical body is no longer radically and deeply revived, nor is it bound to the activity of the protoplasmic energy force of the Essence. This is part of the Divine Plan, so that the soul does not get more tired than it should. So, our physical cover, our physical body deteriorates and is helplessly abandoned by the eternal essence.

Then, the great moment of the deliverance of the soul arrives, accompanied by the acquisition of psychic powers about the people who lived, live and will live on earth. A person's death arrives at a predetermined time and, depending on the person's mission and destination, may be short or long.

How long a soul will remain in the inferior world of physical form, which is our physical world, is engraved on the person's etheric body.

By what we write, the reader must not imagine that we believe that those who commit suicide have the right to be exempt from physical life, especially when it is difficult and leads to a dead end. On the contrary. We are all obliged to follow the ruling of the supreme beings or the White Hierarchy that manage the worlds of lower form to the letter and within the time they have predefined for us.

In order to convince you of this, I consider it my obligation to mention a few extracts – as many as the limited space of a book permits – from the writings of my Master Nikolaos Margioris from his book *The Last Day of Socrates* from the dialogue of Phaidon.

Socrates was waiting for his execution to be carried out. But because the feasts of Delos – where Apollo (spirit) was worshiped by the fathers of the Greeks – were underway and all executions were deferred during the festivities, Socrates had a few more days of life until the ship returned from Delos, marking the end of the feast of Apollo. That was when his students, Cebes and Simmias, asked him about suicide.

He responded that it was in opposition to the divine law and whoever commits suicide will suffer the consequences. Then Cebes said that he had heard the same by Philolaus, but he hadn't heard the why, and that is what he asks Socrates. Then Socrates answered that man was placed in life as a guard and as a custodian of life of his own free will and by Divine Law. How is it possible for someone to abandon his position, which he has accepted voluntarily and of his own free will?

Then, they ask him if a person should feel bitterness when expecting the arrival of death and they mention certain birds that supposedly cry and sing mournfully before their imminent death.

They give the example of the SWAN, which sings one song as it is dying. This is a fact because as a symbol of the God Apollo, who was the patron god of divination, the Swan inherits or acquires the gift of the Oracle.

Then, Socrates answers calmly and peacefully that the Swan and its Swan Song, its last song, is a song of joy and happiness because it knows that it will be freed from the matter keeping it in the physical world – manifestation. When the Swan dies, it will soon after be delivered from the bonds of matter and it will once again find its free course in the world of discarnate existence.

Death is the great end of philosophers or of those

who have found the meaning of life. Whoever has inherited the gift of Divination (Mania) or of prophecy foresees the end of his physical world and of his physical manifestation and takes particular delight in the knowledge, because his soul will reach the Elysian Fields where perfection reigns, where the perfect deceased human beings are drawn.

The matter of death, from an esoteric point of view, is predetermined from the moment of our soul's descent to our dimension and its incarnation. In the etheric body of the being that descends for incarnation, the stages in preparation for death and the end of physical life are predetermined in every detail.

So, when the time approaches, the soul is aware of its deliverance and without wanting to it conveys it to the physical brain, the brain of the person who is dying. This warning is called a Divination and is considered a tragic divination (a subconscious warning). However, deep down, it is the antithesis of life and – why not? – the antithesis of comedy. And that is the tragedy for those who are not cognizant of things.

When the time comes, the soul turns off the tap of life or cuts the frontal or Silver Cord with "scissors". When the tap of the entrance of the Essence of Life (Prana) is turned off, then our physical body is definitely condemned to death.

Death is the abandonment of the physical body

from the cohesive life force of Creation that allows the molecules of matter to disperse. Thus begins the process of de-incarnation of a person, when the entrance for the reason for being in the physical body or in the outermost protective suit of the soul that is passing through is cut off.

It is true that death concerns only our two bodies, the physical and the etheric, since our world consists of two parts, our physical and our etheric world. But these two worlds are composed of two different qualities of matter, which constitute our two bodies, the outermost entities of our spirit-soul. So, the death or transmigration of our soul or the dissolution of the two bodies requires a series of phases, a procedure that has a ritualistic character, because in our world – the physical-etheric or the etheric-physical – absolutely everything is done ritualistically.

This occurs because our soul struggles to remove, to mould or to cohere matter in a proper and constructive way. So, in death, several esoteric rituals have to take place, and their purpose is to release the soul from the two bonds: its physical and its etheric bonds.

There are **seven** phases and the evolved, the mystics, know them and control them or fully comply with them and use them to free themselves as soon as possible.

Let us take a quick look at the **seven phases** of

human death or the dissolution of our physical and then our etheric body.

First Phase: The valve of Sutratma closes.

Second Phase: Depletion of the stored quantity of prana from the centres of power or chakras.

Third Phase: Depletion of the energy accumulated in the seven physical glands of our body.

Fourth Phase: Secretion from the Pineal gland of the euthanasia hormone (hormone of Euthanasia or Deliverance, unknown to science to this day). This hormone is dissolved in the blood and is absorbed by the cells of the physical body, which automatically becomes numb and every pain in the physical body immediately disappears. It is basically a strong drug and poison that facilitates and calms a person before death.

Fifth Phase: Release of the crystallized life force (Kundalini) that is stored in the coccyx, under the Muladhara Chakra that brings and forms the beings of the diaconate and/or the relatives and friends who come to receive the human soul either in the etheric or in the physical world.

Sixth Phase: Cessation of heart function and the necrosis of a person due to the cells that continue to lose the breath of life and are no longer recipients of the etheric cells of prana that give them life.

Seventh Phase: The soul overcomes the obstacles and, taking with it the etheric body, tries to leave and distance itself. But it is held by our etheric net-body that is attracted to an unbelievable degree to the now dead physical body. Finally, at some point, it distances itself little by little from the mortal remains of the departed and the process of dissolution of the etheric body follows.

To the few who are initiated, this dramatic process takes place quickly and without delay. But for the many, it is unbelievably slow. The etheric doesn't want to take leave of its physical mate, which it lived with for so many decades. So it keeps the soul tightly closed within it and tries in vain to convince the soul to turn on the valve that allows entrance of the life force in order to seek its physical mate and resurrect its dead companion. However, the soul works in an organized manner and, little by little, it distances the etheric from the physical dead body.

Despite all this, the soul has not yet been released and remains in its etheric covering above the grave of its buried physical body. But the days pass, they are three days of agony and the soul takes pains to remove itself from the etheric body, the strong tool it possessed in our world in order to control and restrain the physical body. That is what "the thirds" (a third-day memorial service) signify.

The positive thoughts of friends, relatives and acquaintances help release the soul and weaken the etheric body. Quite often, this struggle lasts up to nine days and then "the ninths "take place. In rare cases, this struggle of the soul lasts forty days and in aid of the soul, a memorial service is held on the fortieth day. And that is how the soul is forever released from its etheric-physical adventures.

DEATH AS BENEFACTOR

Death is the most vivid and the most intense phenomenon in the world of form, and it shocks the incarnated souls that remain behind to say farewell to the deceased.

Death is the decomposition, the dematerialization and, above all, it is the departure of the spirit-soul. To die means to abandon one's physical body. At the moment of its abandonment, the soul automatically and under normal conditions enters the adjacent astral dimension where it is projected in another material carrier, the astral carrier or its astral body or its astral cloak.

It is the transition of the soul from the physical pulse-vibration to the astral pulse-vibration. The phenomenon of transition from one dimension to the other is called transmigration. The uninitiated call this transmigration death.

The lack of insight by the vast majority of our fellowmen makes them associate death with loss, destruction, waste. The matter that accommodates us has adopted us and has certain rights over us. It has made us its children,

We know ourselves only by our body, our face and our physiognomy. But these are the products of matter and they disappear as soon as the spirit-soul that forms them departs. The pain is the result of the severance of the relationship between the soul and matter. The Mind marks the pain. The body feels the abnormality of its origin and suffers pain. The soul observes the pain from afar, registering its causes.

Death is the result of the final departure of the soul. Its recovery within a few hours is called a death trance and has absolutely nothing to do with death. Now, death is a benefactor. It is a great esoteric Law that counters the law of life. We have the known pair of life and death. Whoever enters life will leave at some point. They can neither leave life without first entering it, nor can they enter it without ever leaving it.

Upon returning after many years in India, one sage was informed that all his children had died and the answer he gave was the following: *"I knew that I had given birth to mortals, I hadn't given birth to immortals."* Therefore, I know that I came into the world as a mortal. So I expect death as a certainty.

The human pain one suffers as a result of separation due to death occurs because matter suffers when it sees its creation dying. Matter is humbled and humiliated. This produces fear and sadness, deep pain and despair.

Humans, always committed to the exoteric side of

daily life, learn how to appreciate and to handle only the products of the outside world. They find themselves positioned among and socializing with people who are similar to them. Their perception of the things of this world is shared and coordinated. The departure of one of the two brings unhappiness to the one left behind. It is the loss of a companion, a sibling, a parent, a child, one's beloved. Matter has been defeated. The psycho-spiritual being entrapped within it is freed.

Death is the Benefactor of people; that is what was proclaimed during the initiation of the new guides/mystics during the ancient **Eleusinian Mysteries.** During death, the soul abandons its physical body and it goes exactly where its astral body allows it to go. The physical body dissolves into the elements of the physical world of which it was composed.

The spirit-soul, wrapped in the astral protective suit, ascends the sky (the inner dimensions) and arrives in its predefined anchorage. The astral body has a Mind, Intellect and Judgement made up of astral matter. Being more pliable, astral matter produces better organs than what physical matter had to offer. Now the Mind works faster than the former physical Mind.

This new state will not last longer than predefined. The spirit-soul will be re-incarnated and, at some point, will again descend to the thirteenth dimension. It will form an etheric-physical body. It will once again become a tortured person, a mortal. Now, with this incarnation, new hardships begin.

Pain, sighs and a flood of tears. We turn the pages of life, repulsed. There is neither human joy nor happiness. They are relative states only ... This perhaps occurs because no religion has taught the essence of death in depth. Everybody is uninformed and badly orientated concerning the mystery of the human race. The mystery of life and death. The entrance and exit of the spirit-soul from the world of form.

Death is the greatest gift the Creator has granted His creations. The regeneration of the worlds and of the beings relies on death. For wherever it exists, life follows. Life comes from death.

Whoever grasps the meaning of the Laws of Creation will understand the beneficial significance of death. That's why the Hindus cry with birth and rejoice with death. And so, the souls are prepared to accept the greatest sorrow of death – separation – with... stoicism.

The **Esotericist – Metaphysicist** is aware of the cause of things. He cries at death for the separation from his loved ones. Perhaps Karma will separate them for a little while or for many years. It is this physical separation they think of and suffer from.

There are Esoteric Laws concerning life and death that define the time limits in the world of form. The Law of death presupposes knowledge that we common people don't have. None of those who are born will remain untouched by death. Everything that is born will die. When beings ascend to eso-dimensions, inaccessible to matter, then there is no death. Once composed, matter dissolves. The Spirit, the Substance, does not dissolve, does not die, is not composed so as to waste away. With death, life begins. The New life starts from the cold grave. We bless death as a benefactor of the worlds and of the beings.

THE PICTURE ON THE COVER OF THE BOOK *LIFE AFTER DEATH* BY NIKOLAOS MARGIORIS

Ancient Greek amphora from 6th century BC that depicts the death of Sarpedon. A work by Euphronios.

The above picture is on the cover of Nikolaos Margioris' book entitled **Life After Death**, which is a unique and unprecedented **comprehensive treatise** on the subject of the Afterlife. It depicts an **ancient Greek amphora** that was held in a special room in the **Metropolitan Museum of Art** in New York, and is now in the collection of the **National Etruscan Museum**, in the Villa Giulia in Rome. From there we hope it may be returned to Greece again.

The drawing on the amphora is by **Euphronios** and it immortalizes the phenomenon of death. On this amphora from **6th century BC**, the death of Sarpedon is clearly depicted.

Sarpedon was the brother of **Aeacus, Minos** and **Rhadamanthus**. According to Greek Mythology, he was the fourth member of the Karmic Committee, the Holy Committee of the Judges of the Souls, the leaders of Karma, as presumed by Esotericism.

Reference is made to mythological events that tell us great things and give us symbolic information about the subject of death. Euphronios depicts the scene as follows: **Death**, who is looking upwards, comes and takes hold of the upper body of **Sarpedon**.

Sleep comes from below and lifts his legs. Both figures – sleep and death – were personified in order to be more easily perceived by the average person because we must even personify God in order to understand him through anthropomorphic representation.

Our consciousness is unable to understand that the finite of a presentation of form cannot encompass the eternal and infinite that is called Divinity or God in its fullness.

Our smallness wants that they be limited and in accordance with our small soul and imagination; it makes us feel we know and grasp everything and we give God form.

We have the mistaken belief that the morphic presentation controls everything – the infinite, the Flame, the Eternal. It is the Spirit that pervades everything, so much so that the human mind cannot conceive it, detect it, enjoy it, feel it.

Beside **Sleep** and **Death** stands **Hermes** the **soul carrier**, who waits to take the free soul and guide it to where the order of things has determined. Either to the **Elysian Fields** or to **Hades-Pluto**.

This picture that Master **Nikolaos Margioris** placed on the cover of his book *Life After Death* is considered to be one of the greatest philosophic, artistic and metaphysical images that exists, and the time has come for it to be desymbolized so that everyone can benefit from the symbolic and significant truths it hides.

In this depiction, we see **Death** who is guiding the **spiritual part/domain** of man. Death is looking upwards and is holding/pulling Sarpedon up, meaning that it is taking the spiritual place of the deceased in order to help it ascend.

What's more, when the body of the Christian **Saint Patapios** was accidentally found. According to Margioris, Saint Patapios is the writer of Pseudo-Dionysius the Areopagite, the first bishop of Athens. Saint Patapios lived in the 4th century AC in **Loutraki of Corinthia** (in Greece). In 1922, they found his coffin, the upper half of which – the part covering the saint's torso – was made of cedar wood and the bottom half was made of marble. Wood symbolizes the spirit, hence the crucifixion of Jesus Christ on a wooden cross. It symbolizes the path to eternity. And the marble symbolizes matter, heavy matter, the perishable part of the body that follows its own course.

This is additional proof used by the subsequent Christian pantheon that the picture of Euphronios painted in the 6th century BC, shows that the ancient Greeks were initiated in eternity. How wise were these men and how much did they actually know from back then?

Death is the **benefactor** of man because it takes the spirit, the immortal, the eternal, that is found in the chest and guides it to eternity, and the remaining body, the lower part, is led below by **Sleep** that looks downwards, to the earth, to matter and it carries it toward matter, while the **soul carrier Hermes**, as a delegate of the **Divine Authority**, supervises the whole procedure.

It will be our great pleasure to publish the English version of Nikolaos Margioris' *Life After Death* after his children have edited the work, since it constitutes the **most thorough and profound TESTIMONY** concerning the phenomenon of death in its entirety, encompassing the entire range of the eso-depths and the psycho-spiritual course and evolution of the soul until its perfection. This book is a gift for anyone who has the right and wants to gain insight on the matter on a truly experiential metaphysical basis, from the most basic level of a person as a material being to one's highest ascent, facing the Divine Being.

EPILOGUE

We should mention that every effort was made to include as much information as possible as well as the more representative data and details concerning not only the phenomenon of death but also many other issues, all of which are directly related with the evolution of the soul throughout the course of its multiple recyclings through hundreds of carriers, human bodies, which it dons and rejects at regular time intervals, always with regard to one's free will and the karma one has formed and constantly readjusts; and if one is initiated, attempts to polish, to refine and ultimately unburden oneself of.

It is certain that we do not gain exhaustive insight into the subject/matter of death and its purpose or necessity by reading a basic introductory – though substantial – essay concerning the issue, nor can it easily be analysed in depth.

And that's because the details concerning this matter are COUNTLESS, the areas of transmigration and passage or temporary residence of the soul are innumerable, the roles that every separate soul and evolution assume are very different, and finally the human physical mind is of too limited ability and range to conceive and to link events and details that are far more superior to it.

That's why turning to the **Knowledge** of the living **Mystics** and **their students** constitutes an initial **fundamental precondition** for us if we wish to witness the **Correct** and **Original Image of the Truths** that rule **ALL metaphysical phenomena**, whatever they may be, in unison with **ALL physical events**.

Only the **Mystics** are competent and responsible enough to enlighten us about every aspect of metaphysical matters that should interest every being, or will interest them at a given moment, or already interests our fellow beings.

Therefore, if we don't make sure to receive Knowledge from the **Divine Knowledge of the Mystics**, then we will either receive none, or we will receive a distorted version created from our own human imagination or the imagination of third persons or an invented version or a commercialised one by other fellow beings who, in essence, for karmic reasons of evolution for each one separately, but also for their/our marginal evolution, this Knowledge is limited or more or less deviates from the **One original and hyper-substantial**

Knowledge that is grounded and disseminated to our world **ONLY** by the **incarnated Mystics** and less by the **spiritual Masters.**

We must bear in mind that the superior knowledge that our other fellow human beings claim to convey as mediums or communicants or even as meditators, for a number of reasons that we cannot analyse at this moment, is neither comprehensive nor always representative of many aspects of esoteric, let alone spiritual truths, nor is it always accurate, nor original, nor of great importance.

Of course, we are free to hear everything and become informed but we should endeavour to come closer to **the works of the Mystics** and try to see ourselves, our fellowmen, Nature, manifest or unmanifest Creation, the soul, the spirit and the Divine, all possible levels of the ascending evolutionary course through **their psycho-spiritual eyes.**

Let us try to emulate them and we may find we have truly benefitted, as will human society as a whole when its individual members turn to the **One Truth of the Mystics and the Divine.**

Let us step outside the confines of the standard and insufficient exoteric reasoning or the insufficient/ incomplete or even misleading esoteric briefing that remains confined within the restrictive esoteric conceptions of our fellow beings, who are only one step ahead of us and are equally affected and dependent on the same material and etheric-astral matrix of the universe world, on their own moderate level of spiritual evolution, and mainly on their own karmic settlements and motives or personal or commercial interests.

Only in this way will we give ourselves profoundly more authentic opportunities and true potential to unravel the real psycho-spiritual forces and exercise our right to the Truth and to the Divine Being and to our real destination and duty.

The responsibility of upgrading and confirming all superior philosophical theories is always ultimately in our own hand, dependent on our own participation, through the practices of true **meditation** or true **mysticism** that lead us to the personal actualization of our own worth and to an essential acceptance of spiritual evolution.

We wish that for everyone, body and soul.

EPILOGUE OF THE ENTIRE WORK

Esotericism, without being bound by dogmas and religious – ecclesiastic limits, teaches, analyses, experiments, proves and analytically interprets symbols, traditions and myths through the philosophical approaches of all the great mystics of humanity.

Although it regards faith as a primary force of ascension, it also recognizes that faith alone is not enough. It must be coupled with esoteric knowledge. Then, and only then, will our faith have the foundations to stand on and will the mysteries on earth become reality.

Esotericism travels deeper into the preternatural, the unknown and secret mysteries of the unified world – universe and it explores the causes and the hidden laws and it finds a way to answer the numerous questions and it always gives explanations for the incomprehensible mysteries that our own nature hides.

It studies the psychical phenomena unceasingly, without prejudice, fanaticism and superstition. It particularly deals with the invisible worlds hidden to the senses, before the sheer scale of which we are but a drop in the ocean.

Esotericism encompasses within it all the teachings of all religions, of the new and the ancient world, and it has the one and only God as its primary philosophical belief.

It believes and gradually perceives the existence of invisible worlds, which it concedes are governed by a great morality, which is supervised by an order of beings who are spiritually superior to us here on earth.

This hyper-moral order is a universal principle that jointly works with others in the eso-universes and together they guide all morphic creations of the inner and outer world.

It is this moral order that religion professes and tries, in its own way, to dogmatically and despotically enforce in our materialistic life. By teaching this sense of morality, every religion hopes to achieve two and perhaps three results.
1) Earthly bliss.
2) The obligatory contact of the worshipper with a superior and divine justice.
3) The hope of a speedy deliverance from our known material life that is futile and barren.

When Religion or Philosophy (Esotericism, to be more specific) manages to realize this dream; that is, to draw the attention of people from the pettiness of our life on earth and to orientate them towards the Superior, the Celestial, the Spiritual, the incomparable in Beauty Eso-systems of the pulse-depth, then two pleasant events must occur on our pain-causing earth.

First: Wealth and glory will be left behind as useless and dangerous and automatically our unworthy and futile problems will be solved.

Second: Hostility and hatred, lust and passion will be wiped out from our life and a peaceful life born of eternal real love will reign on earth.

From the moment we turn our gaze toward the great Truth, an unforgettable dawn will brighten our soul, a joy of deliverance will embrace the world and the enslaved love will pour out from the human soul.

It is in the hope of this great dawn that **Nikolaos Margioris**, the contemporary Greek mystic, and his students have invested what powers they possess since very early on.

It is with these powers that he taught the secret belief of his soul, with which any seeker will easily find the yarn that will lead to freedom from the deep darkness of the labyrinth of a material life.

It is in this direction of high spiritual worth that all we, his students, work hoping to open-handedly spread the enormous and rare wealth of the esoteric and spiritual experiential knowledge of our Master to the whole universe.

CURRICULUM VITAE OF
ILIAS KATSIAMPAS

Ilias L. Katsiampas was born on October 30th 1965 in Trikala of Thessaly (Greece) where he grew up and lives today. He is a graduate of Physical Education (TEFAA), he has worked as a journalist for the last twenty-two years and he is the writer and publisher of 15 philosophical works. He is married to Sofia A. Skoumi, with whom he has two children, Lampros and Maria.

From a very young age, he expressed a strong esoteric interest in seeking the essence of things, the real meaning of life. He studied many philosophical systems as well as volumes of books on Esotericism of every kind, from different times and countries, until he met **Nikolaos A. Margioris, the Greek Master of Esotericism** (1913-1993), in whose spiritual work he recognized the presence of substantial Knowledge, the supreme real truth. He became his student and remained close to him from 1983 until his physical passing on May 6th 1993.

Among other things, he received training in the pure form of Raja Yoga and in numerous other esoteric fields of interest (Esoteric Philosophy, Esoteric Theology, Mysticism, Astrology-Astrosophy, Hypnotism-Orthopsychism, Scientific Spiritualism, Esoteric Therapeutics, etc.) and gradually ascended the steps of his spiritual evolution.

The fiery and indomitable tendency and willingness of the writer to explore the Beyond in combination with his extensive training, apprenticeship and direct close relationship with his Master, N. Margioris, for almost a decade contributed decisively to the gradual formation of his clear integrated experiential perception-point of view on the whole field of Metaphysics, as well as on the practices of meditation and mysticism.

On **January 18, 1992**, with the full encouragement, guidance and in the presence of his Master, he inaugurated the **Omakoio of Trikala**, an educational-spiritual centre, where all the **Yoga** systems (Mantram, Kriya, Raja, Karma, Jnani, Bhakti, Kundalini, Sahaja, Atmoliquefaction), **Esoteric Philosophy, Alternative** and **Esoteric Therapeutics** and generally **Esotericism** (Occultism and Mysticism) are taught to this day.

Since 1999, he has been active in the **Omakoio of Thessaloniki.**

In **July 2012**, along with his partners and students, he established the Association "YOGA ACADEMY OF NIKOLAOS MARGIORIS-OMAKOIO" as a tribute to his Master, **N. Margioris**, for a more holistic application of his philosophical and practical work.

He proclaims and highlights the paramount need for the widespread teaching of **Esotericism** (Introversion – Self-Knowledge) in order to create healthy and balanced minds and a truly New Spiritual Man characterized by self-awareness, self-reliance, autonomy, an open mind, a giving disposition free of materialistic pettiness and repressed desires, and an ability to better adapt and respond to the challenges of modern reality as well as to every future time of Humanity.

SHORT BIOGRAPHICAL NOTE ON PYTHAGORAS AND ON NIKOLAOS MARGIORIS OR "THE OMAKOIO OF PYTHAGORAS AND THE WORK OF NIKOLAOS MARGIORIS"

Written by **Ilias L. Katsiampas** (*)

The word **Omakoio** is a composite of – *omou* (together) we hear. We hear high exoteric, esoteric and spiritual teachings (*om-akouein*, we hear the OM, the perfect sound).

It is the great Greek philosopher and mystic **Pythagoras**, who first used the word **Omakoio** or **Omakoeio** in the 6th century BC, establishing a school of the same name in **Croton** of Southern Italy, the Great Greece of the time.

Pythagoras was a **great spiritual figure** (see the books *Pythagorean Philosophy, The Two-Volume Metaphysical Encyclopaedia* and *Occultism (Occultology)- Volume B,* by Nikolaos A. Margioris, Omakoio of Athens Editions), of **universal renown and merit**, whose contribution to nearly all branches of art, science and spirituality was immense, diachronic, pan-human.

Édouard Schuré, in his famous work *The Great Initiates,* cites **Pythagoras** among the Eight Great Mystics of humanity who enrich the spiritual greatness and the benefaction of man.

When his mother went to the **Oracle of Delphi** to ask about her forthcoming birth, the **Pythia** said to her, *"You will bear a son who will be useful to all men for all time."*

Pythagoras was born in **Samos** and from a very young age he was fortunate enough to become acquainted with many Teachers (Hermodamas, Pherecydes, the Ionian Philosophers), and witness many initiations (Heraian Mysteries) before he decided, at the age of 22, to travel to the sister country, Egypt (see the book *Dravidians, the Ancestors of the Greeks, Egyptians and Hindus* by N. Margioris, *The Reign of*

Minos, the Great King of Crete as well as *The Pharaohs Akhenaten and Tutankhamun*, Omakoio of Athens Editions) in order to continue his initiation.

After a stay of 22 years, he managed to reach the last seventh degree of the Secretary of the Temples that made him the equal and successor of the Archpriest of Egypt. After several adventures, one of which was being held captive by the Persian King Cambyses and imprisoned in dungeons for many years, he was called upon to heal the wife of the king in exchange for his freedom. Without delay, he returned to his country, Samos.

With his vast knowledge and his multifaceted personal experiences, he travelled across a large part of Greece and gradually revived or reinforced the most important ancient Greek mysteries among which are the Eleusinian Mysteries, the Idaean, the Epidauria, the Mysteries of Delphi, in which he is even considered to have confided the secret of atomic energy in extremely simple terms, thus enabling the priests to defend themselves against the invading Persians by successfully striking them down at least twice.

He provided the means for the **Pythia, the oracles** of Delphi, to become infallible and he trained the priestess **Theoclea** to this end. She reached her zenith, and in the presence of other priests and Pythagoras – who guided her – she foretold the bleak future of Greece, of Pythagoras himself and his forthcoming incarnation as the Word.

In fact, when **Pythagoras** arrived in **Eleusis** and assisted as an honoured guest in the **Eleusinian Mysteries** or the Initiations for the cult of Mother and Kore (Demeter or Mother or Consciousness or Matter and Persephone or Kore or Subconsciousness or Soul), the great **Hierophant Nikokleas** invited him to accept the mighty sceptre of the Eleusinian Mysteries and to continue the initiation himself (Pythagoras) and to converse with the prospective overseers (see the books of Nikolaos Margioris *The Pharaohs Akhenaten and Tutankhamun*, and *Eleusinian Mysteries*, Omakoio of Athens editions).

After spending two years in Delphi foreseeing the future, he left for the colonies of the then flourishing Magna Graecia (Great Greece) and chose to go to **Croton**, to the greatest and most glorified state. There he appealed to the senate and asked for permission to create his school. Soon he was accused of atheism and corruption by some of his rivals and enemies and he found himself apologizing to the Council of One Thousand. There, for almost two and half days, he orated his dream and what he wanted to do for Greece. He converted nearly all his enemies into friends, and quite a few even became his students.

He created the first **Open Community University – School** in the **Universe**, the like of which has never existed since nor is likely to exist in the future.

He gave it the name **Omakoeio** or **Omakoio** and thousands of his students lived there, on their own or with their families, following the systematic intellectual and practical training he open-handedly offered them. This **endeavour** is a **unique example** of an open educational institution of such a large scale making scientific teachings (exoteric, esoteric and spiritual) accessible and understandable to humanity.

After systematic studies of over a decade, those who graduated were entitled to establish similar schools wherever they wished to teach.

Where to begin when it comes to Pythagoras and his teachings? It was as if God descended on earth and gave this man all the wealth of Wisdom, Perfection, Beauty and Truth.

He was **blessed by God**. Everything started from Pythagoras. Before him, there was nothing specific. **He specified everything**. He was the leader. We relied on him.

A fresh breeze of knowledge, truth, humanity and spirituality blew in his time and it contributed to the transformation of many people who voluntarily chose to delve deeply into the truths of life. A new foundation was sowed. The Greek race, with the contribution of Pythagoras and Socrates, Plato, Heraclitus, Anaximenes, Thales and many others, reached its spiritual zenith.

The **Omakoio** was unique in that, for the first time in human history, Scientific and Theological teaching or thorough and deep studies of the Visible and the

Invisible World took place at the same time. It was here that the **Tetragram (Tetraktys)**, the sacred symbol the **Pythagoreans** swore oaths by, was introduced. It was the tool of measurement and expansion of the Worlds and the Beings.

He discovered a system of tuning and a musical scale, the monochord, the polychord, the harmony of the spheres, therapeutics, astrology – astronomy (he taught the heliocentric theory), human physiognomy, art, agriculture, poetry, metal works, goldsmithing, drama, comedy, tragedy, gymnastics, nutrition and other fields.

Furthermore, today's sciences – mathematics, geometry, medicine, theology and philosophy – all derive from Pythagoras. His teachings were Infinite and the influence he exerted great.

He was the first to possess the secret of the **Divine Existence** of the unique and the Monad. He preached **Monotheism** through numbers behind closed doors. **He became the Spiritual Father of the WHOLE of humanity.**

He was the **sun** that came to enlighten the world, because the **Word** was following behind him and he had to open the way in order that the people could comprehend the words of the Kingdom of the Heavens.

He was gifted with incomparable clairaudient and clairvoyant abilities as well as intuition, but he also had many other qualities. He succeeded in uniting the Sky and the Earth and retaining this union on his own.

The **Omakoio** of **Croton**, through the words of **Pythagoras** and with thousands of boarders-students, managed to solve the problems of all people and of all times. Not only because it gave us the bases and the guidelines for all the sciences and the arts that have burgeoned and developed immensely in our times, but mainly for the **spiritual reform** of humanity.

If his manifold work, which in essence was the metamorphosis of man from within to protypical psycho-spiritual standards, had not been abruptly discontinued, there is no doubt that humanity would have followed another, more qualitative, more authentic and more substantial path towards evolution than the one it is following nowadays. One that would have been closer to the esoteric truth.

The **spiritual beacon** that lit up for the first time (postdiluvian) in the Universe to lead the navigators or the human souls was unfortunately destroyed by fire and sword.

Cylon (*Occultology – Volume B*, by N. Margioris, *Omakoio* magazine and others), a student who failed to attain the initial admission requirements for the Omakoio, became a bitter politician and demagogue, who worked methodically and misleadingly for many years in order to defame and demolish what Pythagoras had created.

Finally, under special circumstances, he achieved his purpose and, one night, along with a congregation of his fanatic adherents, he burnt down the Omakoio and killed most of Pythagoras' students and staff. It is said that Pythagoras, his wife and some of his disciples escaped and lived for many more years in Metapontum, where he died.

His work was continued by his wife Theano, who in order to survive, resold many of the notes he kept to Plato, who went to Metapontum for this reason alone. Using these notes, Plato wrote his Platonic Philosophy, which is inseparable from the man.

Certain of Pythagoras' disciples who were rescued escaped to Greece. Among them was **Lysis**, who went to Thebes and became the Teacher of Epaminondas; **Archippos**, who later became Plato's assistant and elderly Teacher; **Philolaus**; **Alkaios the doctor** who was one of the supervisors who taught Hippocrates and others.

Also, Neo-Pythagoreanism and Neo-Platonism constituted the mediaeval mystic orders of Europe as well as of the East.

Pythagoras wanted to form a new society based on the Esoteric Truths and on the fixed eternal invisible Laws.

It seems that he succeeded in doing so for the approximately thirty (30) years that his Omakoio functioned. He instilled the esoteric truth in the souls of his disciples, he created worthy teachers and he earned the admiration and the interest not only of the men of his time but also of all time...

May we have the strength and maturity to emulate him as individuals and as a society.

THE WORK OF NIKOLAOS MARGIORIS AND THE OMAKOIOS

The modern Greek mystic Nikolaos Margioris

2500 years after the analytical and multidimensional, theoretical and practical, experiential teaching approach of the great and inimitable spirit of **Pythagoras**, **Nikolaos A. Margioris** (1914-1993), the contemporary experiential esoteric philosopher and christocentric mystic arrived to leave his mark on this world.

Born in 1913 in **Samos**, he travelled, lived and studied in **India**, **Tibet** and **Egypt** for many years, returning to **Greece** in **1958** and settling in Athens.

During this time, he chanced upon great masters (Baba, Krino Andre Salvatore De Castro, Greek orthodox patriarchs) while at the age of nearly 13 he had his first fully **spiritual** experience (Samadhi -Theosis) which he describes in the epilogue of his book *Raja Yoga, elevation of the mind from the conscious to the hyper-conscious.*

There followed many frequent deliverance-type of elevations, through which he managed to ground important esoteric and spiritual knowledge, truths and... revelations on a plethora of crucial human, esoteric and highly spiritual issues.

The most important of all in duration and in esoteric spiritual fullness was the one that lasted for nearly **thirty** days, the **Nirguna Samadhi-Theosis**, during which he not only traversed the eso-depth of Creation but he was also able to approach the **Divine Side...** These Cosmogonic, Apocalyptic and Revelatory events-experiences are described in his books *The Birth and Death of the Worlds, matter, anti-matter, hyper-matter; Esoteric Philosophy* and *Life After Death.*

He has also made **esoteric contact** with many **great spiritual Teachers,** some of whom we **only indicatively** mention: **Saint Patapios** (according to Margioris, he is the one who wrote the Pseudo-Dionysius the Areopagite that was translated into Latin by Eriugena in 850AD, which imparted the fire of mysticism in Europe. Details are divulged in his first book entitled *Patapios, the Humble Philosopher and Saint from Egypt),* **Ramakrishna, Pythagoras, Saint-Germain,** and among others, **Helena Petrovna Blavatsky,** with whom he often conversed in his sleep and in his awake and whom he called "his mother".

In **1972**, he founded the **Association of Saint Patapios** in Athens, to which he dedicated countless hours until the end of his life delivering free lectures and seminars, organizing educational excursions and other activities.

In **1976**, in honour of **Pythagoras** and in an attempt to revive **Pythagorean views** and **practices**, he founded the **Omakoio of Athens**, an educational and spiritual centre in which he committed himself to disseminating all possible philosophical and practical knowledge that would be of benefit to modern man. In **1990**, he inaugurated the **Omakoio of Lamia**, run by his student Dimitris Tsaparas and in **1992**, the **Omakoio of Trikala**, run by his student Ilias Katsiampas. After his transmigration, his assistant Smaro Kosmaoglou assumed responsibility for the Omakoio of Athens while many new Omakoios were gradually established.

As a **Greek Orthodox**, he also tried to explore the nexus between the orthodox movement, monasticism and mysticism in the deserts of Egypt during the 3rd and 4th century AD and eastern metaphysical philosophy. **Christopher II**, the blessed Patriarch of Alexandria, guided him on these philosophic searches and for years put him to work in the Orthodox libraries of the Patriarchate of Alexandria and of Saint Catherine's Monastery in the Sinai Desert. The Patriarch spent many hours discussing with his student of the time. He honoured him with his friendship and he bestowed the **Cross** of **Saint Marc** upon him for his contribution to the **Church** and to the **Patriarchate of Alexandria and all Africa**. His successor, the blessed Patriarch **Nicholas VI**, did the same.

Undoubtedly, he was a rare, charismatic and multi-talented figure, a dynamic and prolific writer who produced an unprecedented body of work on contemporary esoteric experiences, which silently spread beyond the threshold of our country (Greece), delivering the quintessence of his accomplished spiritual experiences.

Between **1970** and **1993**, he devoted countless hours teaching his multifaceted wisdom, all the while writing and editing a total of **189 works** on various subjects.

His written work can be separated into books pertaining to **history – pre-history, ancient Greece;** and **the occult, science, alternative and esoteric therapeutics, systems and practices** of **yoga;** and **mysticism, occultology, esoteric theology;** and **philosophy, De-symbolism of Greek mythology, meditation, ancient Greek Asclepean massage** and **sleeping therapy (contemporary hypnotism), scientific spiritualism, the philosophy** of **astrology, esoteric initiation** and so on.

Among his works, it is worth making special mention of the *The Two-Volume Metaphysical Encyclopaedia; the Eleusinian Mysteries; Dravidians, the Ancestors of Greeks; The Reign of Minos, the Great King of Crete; Hatha Yoga; Kriya Yoga; Karma and Raja*

Yoga; The Pharaohs Akhenaten and Tutankhamun – with a method to learn Hieroglyphic Writing; The Chiroplastic Therapeutics of SHIATSU; Psychotherapeutics without Medication; The Birth and Death of the Worlds; Life After Death; Mystical Teachings; Patapios, the Humble Philosopher and Saint from Egypt; Christocentric and Christocratic Mysticism; The Other View of Erich Von Daniken's Dogma; Light in the Dark and many others. (www.omakoio.gr).

In fact, just 23 years after his physical end, many are the **distinguished writers and students** who have consulted and have repeatedly used material from his books, making **special mention** of it in their **bibliography**. His articles and other works are in the process of being translated into the English language.

His complete works raised, nurtured, formed and brought to maturity a large part of the Greek society that was freely exploring the spiritual at a time when there was still ignorance and deep... darkness, many superstitions and reproach for esoteric matters and for those who occupy themselves with them in modern Greece.

Margioris' teachings chiefly consist of the **harmonic coexistence** of the **ancient Greek, Egyptian and Hindu philosophic approaches** with the **esoteric Christian tradition**, through the filter of his personal actualization. At the same time, it provides **thorough personal answers** with **unprecedented analyses** on the **Cosmogonic, Ontological** and **Eschatological Matter**, a result of his own **"secret life"**.

The **exoteric, esoteric** and **spiritual contribution** of **Nikolaos Margioris** can be summarized in the general areas below:

He has produced an unprecedented body of **written work** comprising 35 books, 35 essays, 49 issues of the **Omakoio** magazine, 8 well-documented branches of correspondence courses with **10 to 11** extensive **graded written lectures** for every branch and an **INEXAUSTIBLE supply of oral revelatory teaching** that, under certain conditions, is the equivalent of thousands of books.

The size and wealth of **his pure mystic Experiences.** Parts of them are described in his book *Esoteric and Mystic Experiences of Nikolaos A. Margioris.* The climax of these experiences is depicted in the **30-day Nirguna Samadhi-Theosis** described in his books (see his works *The Birth and Death of the Worlds and of the Beings, Life After Death* and *Esoteric Philosophy*) and his corresponding oral revelatory teachings.

He stratified his Occult experiences and provided erudite **systematic metaphysical teachings – analyses** as a result of his personal experiences and knowledge. Among them, we include his theoretical and practical teachings through correspondence course in the following branches of **Esotericism:**

Hypnotism-Orthopsychism: A full theoretical and practical course on three basic systems of hypnotism and explanations for many others. It also discloses rare specialized details concerning the systematic and responsible training for any interested party.

Scientific Spiritualism: Analysis of the prerequisites for making sound, controlled and serious qualitative contact with the invisible and a plethora of relevant details and specialized analyses.

Esoteric Therapeutics: A unique book that compares and contrasts the interaction of esoteric with exoteric - scientific therapeutics, chakras, endocrine glands, hormones, life, death, yoga, kundalini, Sutratma, antahkarana and so on.

Astrology-Astrosophy: Wisdom drawn from the oblivion of the lost ancient Egyptian Horoscope, the Karmic approach and, more specifically, a presentation of the Revelatory Philosophy of Astrology that is absent from most books of this type.

Meditation: A full analysis of all the relevant matters and the specific self-enhancing qualities of meditation that is further discussed and developed in his books *Raja Yoga, Kriya Yoga, The Secret of Hatha Yoga, Karma, Reincarnation* and others.

Esoteric Initiation: A description of initiation rituals-knowledge throughout the ages (antediluvian and postdiluvian), what type of initiations exist, what they involve, how and when they are performed and other relevant information.

Esoteric Philosophy: A revelatory, analytical look at Creation and – as much as possible – at the... Creator.

Desymbolism: The desymbolism and demythologization

of Greek Mythology and many other related matters. Lectures on the seven keys of Desymbolism of Greek Mythology and analytical explanations for the first three of them: an exoteric key, an esoteric key and a compound key, etc.

He **MADE PUBLIC** his great **Revelatory Spiritual Vision** concerning the stratification of Creation from the **Divine Darkness** to **man** and from man to the **Creator**.

Still, when **Occultism** (Occultology) and **Mysticism** (Theosis – Spirituality) are integrated into one person, then a spiritually integrated being we call a **MYSTIC** stands before us and grounds the hyper-substantial truths of Creation to the present world of chronicity that has an **expiry date**.

He offered us his extensive and profound **presentation** of the **esoteric psychophysiology** of important **practices** (**Meditation and Mysticism**) that everyone can use according to their psychosynthesis to accelerate their evolution and acquire a healthy, balanced and highly demanding and distinguished Mind that will cooperate impeccably with its transcendental entity – origin and will be activated to the extreme in our world in order to bring about a healthy grounding of an existent **Divine Plan**.

Nikolaos Margioris offered practical assistance to the **world** with **KRIYA YOGA** (a method of psychosomatic therapeutics – treatment – harmony) that he revived through a Samadhi he achieved for this purpose and brought it back for daily use by people so that they can improve their physical and mental health and treat many contemporary health problems. This subject is developed in a book of the same title.

He introduced the study of **RAJA** and **KUNDALINI YOGA,** which are systematically taught in almost all his Schools, as well as all the basic fundamental kinds of Yoga (Karma, Gnani, Bhakti, Mantram, Kriya, yoga for children) with thorough and extensive analyses and with the corresponding mental exercises. An important reference book is his book *Raja Yoga, elevation of the mind from the conscious to the hyper-conscious.*

Finally, he introduced a **pioneering** system of **detoxification, WEIGHT LOSS and SLIMMING** that he himself invented and called **Atmoliquefaction**, which doesn't use mechanical means and medicines, and which is based on the principles and the practices of Yoga with exceptionally effective results.

He played a great role in **REVIVING** important mild **alternative therapeutic methods** (Esoteric Therapeutics) from antiquity, among which is ancient Greek Asclepean massage, ancient Greek sleep therapy (contemporary hypnotism), magnetotherapy (nowadays it is called bio-energy and/or Reiki, without it being identified with his method), suggestion and other methods.

Also, he **INVENTED** and **used** mild **physiotherapeutic esoteric means** such as Finger-tapping, Glossotherapy, the transfusion of energy, the bio-energetic influence on the chakras (centres of strength) and others, and finally, he played a role in the systematization and classification-grouping of the Japanese Therapeutic **Shiatsu** (Finger-tapping) for the treatment of **186** ailments, of Static and Kinetic Therapeutics, of Reflexology, of Iconoplastic Therapeutics, of ectoplasmatic effusions and many other techniques.

He disclosed a large part of the **occult** (antediluvian and postdiluvian) **history** of man.

He provided **esoteric explanations** of the **Eleusinian Mysteries** of ancient Greece, of the **Asclepean** and **Amfiaraea**, of **the Oracle of Trophonius**, of **Egyptian Initiations** and of other forgotten knowledge, only traces of which have reached our days (Aladdin-style oil lamps, precious stones, the curse of the Pharaohs, the Sphinx, the Pyramids, mummies, space travel... and others). Also, he provided esoteric explanations of the **Greek fire-walkers (Anastenarides)** and of the phenomenon as a whole.

He is largely responsible for today's **relationship** between scientists and metaphysicists, which is the result of contemporary revelations of science that have borrowed from and confirm the age-long experiential tradition and its views. It is written, among others, in his book *Three-dimensional and Four-dimensional World*.

He has contributed to the subject of **extra-terrestrials** with many details and analyses that concern them and ... us, and to relevant subjects that may be of an urgent nature.

He has contributed to the **dissemination** of many **revelatory esoteric pearls of wisdom** that may, if collected and appreciated correctly, prove useful for the developing **sciences** and provide guidance as to what direction new discoveries must take and where to focus their energy and effectiveness. These subjects concern **anti-matter** and **hyper-matter, Supernova**, the chemical element **Argon**, parallel universes, black holes, neutrinos, and other matters.

He has deeply delved into and extensively analysed the **esoteric**, and especially the **mystical experiences** and the **exceptional ascension** (based on their idiosyncrasy and their special psychical evolution) of many worthy children of humanity, among whom are:

Hermes Trismegistus (thrice-greatest), *Akhenaten*, *Pythagoras*, *Plato*, *Ammonius Saccas*, *Plotinus*, *Moses*, *Ramakrishna*, *Vivekananda*, *Paul the Apostle*, *John the Apostle*, *Adamantius Origen the Christian*, *Theofilos Kairis*, *Saint Gregory of Sinai*, *Gregory Palamas* (of the Uncreated Light), *Cosmas of Aetolia*, *Saint Patapios*, *Saint-Germain*, *Alessandro Cagliostro*, *Theophrastus Paracelsus*, *Doctor Papus* (Gérard Encausse), *the Dalai Lama* and others.

He has made a clear **experiential and well-defined distinction** between dreams, visions, intuition, psychometrics, clairaudience, clairvoyance, insight, out-of-body experiences (subconscious), hyper-intellectual function (hyper-consciousness), Samadhi within context and Samadhi out of context (the Sanskrit terms are analysed in the book with the title *From the Master's Mouth to the Student's Ear with a thorough **glossary of Sanskrit** (400 words) for the students of Yoga).*

Apart from everything else, he has also made distinctions and **fully noted, recorded and analysed**, through the light of his actualization, nearly **every metaphysical term-meaning**, in his books *Light in the Dark* and *The Two-Volume Metaphysical Encyclopaedia*, in the *49 issues* of his magazine *Omakoio*, as well as in his student's, Ilias Katsiampas, analytical and revelatory 400- page book titled *Deep Metaphysical Correspondence*.

In February of 2009, **Nikolaos Margioris** ranked **60th** among the **100 Great Greeks of all times** in a public vote that the television channel **SKAI** carried out in April 2008. This was followed by the publication of a **three-volume book**, as well as DVDs, which analytically presented the 100 Great Greeks.

He stood among the **100 Great Greeks** as a result of his contribution to the **formation, presentation** and **popularization** of a contemporary **Greek Metaphysical Philosophy** based on the comparative analysis of the main international philosophical approaches on this subject matter with the equivalent Greek and Christian theories. And he systematically voiced his views about the theoretical and practical ways in which the contemporary Greek (but also every person) can **redefine** his **spiritual course** and **evolution** in the actual environment of corruption and total social decomposition. His contribution is evident in his **189 books** and in his multifaceted and invaluable salvaged oral **testimonies** and **teachings**.

Similar interviews – Extensive Dedications have been published in the **September – October 2002** issue of the magazine *Avaton*, where he is hailed as a "**christocentric mystic**"; in the magazine *Third Eye*, **December 1992** issue, where he is addressed as the **Patriarch of Greek Metaphysical Philosophy**; as well as in the issues of **September 1993** and subsequently in the **May 2004** issue; in the magazine supplement *Phenomena* of the daily newspaper *Eleftheros Typos*; in the magazine *Yoga*, issue of **October 2008** and **January 2010**; on **websites, in interviews** and **books** by many other writers who have drawn material from his work, the books of his students and elsewhere.

He left behind him **an immense** and **diachronic wealth of testimonies** (theoretical and practical) for **study** and **exploitation**. In fact, the ACADEMY OF MARGIORIS – OMAKOIO was established by his students with the purpose of saving, preserving and promoting all this valuable material and they decided to devote themselves to studying, teaching and propagating his work.

His **philosophical** and **practical work** is continued by the Schools **Omakoios** that he founded, as well as by the **newer Schools** established after his death all over Greece, while **his books** are being promoted by his natural heirs through the Omakoios and it is hoped that they will soon be available through Amazon and other websites internationally. His students and representatives will continue publishing newer books based on his oral testimonies and teachings, along with teaching his work.

Apart from the philosophical schools that he himself founded: **Omakoio of Athens, Omakoio of Lamia** and **Omakoio of Trikala**, the following went into operation afterwards: **Omakoio of Thessaloniki, Pythagorean Omakoio, Omakoio of Corinth – Loutraki, Omakoio of Komotini, Omakoio of Rhodes, Omakoio of Karditsa, Omakoio of Piraeus, Omakoio of Corfu and Glyfada.**

Additional information about the writings and the remaining work of N. Margioris at www.omakoio.gr E-mail: omakoio@omakoio.gr or omakoio@gmal.com

See also **two** relevant **interviews** that his student and associate, **Ilias Katsiampas**, gave on his website **Esoterica.gr** and that have been posted at the following electronic address:

http://www.esoterica.gr/podium/interviews/katsiaba/katsiaba.htm

http://www.esoterica.gr/forums/topic.asp?TOPICID=4103

(*) **Ilias L. Katsiampas** is a professor of physical education, a journalist, a writer and an editor. For a decade, he was a student-associate of N. Margioris and he is responsible for the Omakoios of Trikala and Thessaloniki and president of the Yoga Academy of Nikolaos Margioris – Omakoio (www.omakoio.gr, e-mails: omakoio@omakoio.gr omakoeio@gmail.com).

SUMMARY OF THE WORK

The present book examines the great and perennial subject of post-mortem life. It is a deep and detailed approach on the matter of death based on the experiences of great spirits of humanity and it mainly draws on the knowledge provided by the testimonies of the revealed knowledge and integrated personal experiences of the contemporary Greek philosopher, spiritual Master and mystic, **Nikolaos Margioris (1913-1993)**, the writer of more than **180 metaphysical and practical works** and the Master of **great spiritual testimonies** he left behind him.

Throughout the present work, the esoteric experiential truth of life in its own psychospiritual way will accompany us with the eyes of the sixth sense, the soul and the spirit. Our narration will examine the primary role of clairvoyance, intuition, and various out-of-body experiences of the soul and of the spirit (Samadhi, Theosis) throughout the entire spectrum of esoteric Creation, but will mostly focus on the phenomenon of post-mortem life, its stages, the pathogenic states of those departing as well as of those remaining behind, the basic dimensions the average human soul will travel through, the areas it deserves to be and every detail worth mentioning and that may be of value in the enlightenment of every person. Whether this is the first time some readers turn their attention to the subject of post-mortem life or they are expanding existing information and knowledge they may have drawn from various sources, this book will prove a worthy read.

BOOK REVIEW OF
THE MYSTERY OF DEATH
AND THE POST-MORTEM COURSE
OF THE SOUL

Dear Ilias,

I read your new book entitled *The Mystery of Death and the Post-Mortem Course of the Soul*, and I enjoyed it very much. Of course, I have to re-read it many times in order to be able to enjoy it even more.

It is a complete, concise, and profound work that contains everything one needs to know about this extremely sensitive topic that concerns everyone.

A **metaphysical treatise** that adds to our incredibly materialistic world, it presents masterfully woven sparks of knowledge and wisdom on the occultism and mysticism of major mystics, and especially those following the Christian and Hellenocentric ideal, who confirm that the existence of the human spiritsoul is eternal and resembles a boat that travels back and forth between the lower worlds, until it decides to shed some of its load in order to sail even deeper into the crystal clear waters of the inner dimensions and even to its spiritsoul's seat-origin.

The definition of many concepts and terms is given with clarity, and with your profound but simply presented analysis, it becomes directly accessible to those who have little information on the subject. However, those who are knowledgeable on the subject will become better acquainted with the worldview not only of our Christocentric and Christocratic Mystic Nicholaos Margioris, but of other important Mystics, as well as of other great Truths about this huge issue.

The interpretation of the painting on the front cover of the Master's book *Metathanatia Zoi* [*Life After Death*] creates another strong link for the reader between the unique analysis contained in the aforementioned book and, of course, your wonderful and well-rounded approach.

I congratulate you on your working tirelessly, overcoming the obstacles lying in your way, to promote the multifaceted work of our beloved Master, his deeper personality, and also the continuity of his diverse and inspired work in Greece and abroad.

Niki Foufa
Administrator of the Omakoio of Loutraki

SCHOOLS IN OPERATION AT THE OMAKOIOS OF ATHENS, LAMIA AND TRIKALA

For the purpose of informing our readers, we would like to draw their attention to the existence and operation of three Genuine and Autonomous Metaphysical Schools (with an extensive didactic curriculum on Esotericism) which were created in the Greek area and inaugurated by the Master himself. They are the **Omakoio of Athens**, the **Omakoio of Lamia** and the **Omakoio of Trikala**.

We mention them because all three belong to Master Nikolaos A. Margioris' students-instructors, they were established with his full consent and at his urging while he was still alive, and they follow his own Spiritual Legacy and Teachings.

Certainly, every Omakoio always constitutes a Separate and Autonomous Entity-Spiritual School with its own Identity-History and Work and with its own Personality and Instructor.

At the same time, all of them are under the Protection of the Master but also in a Pythagorean Union **(Pythagorean Contact)** among themselves, while each takes care of and serves the individualized liberal philosophical work that it has undertaken under His command.

OMAKOIO OF ATHENS
SMARO I. KOSMAOGLOU
METAPHYSICAL STUDIES IN YOGA AND SHIATSU
ATHENS, GREECE

OMAKOIO OF LAMIA
DIMITRIS & KULA TSAPARA
METAPHYSICAL STUDIES IN YOGA AND SHIATSU
LAMIA, GREECE

OMAKOIO OF TRIKALA
ILIAS L. KATSIAMPAS
METAPHYSICAL STUDIES IN YOGA AND SHIATSU
21 KEFALLINIAS STREET
42131 TRIKALA, GREECE
TEL. & FAX: 0030-24310-75505
& MOBILE: 0030-6974-580768
Web site: http://www.omakoio.gr
E-mails: omakoio@omakoio.gr & omakoeio@gmail.com

Recently, individual efforts are also being expended to make His Work more widely known with the operation – apart from everything else - of new branches in various parts of Greece.

The Omakoio of Athens is extending its activities to Piraeus with a branch that will be under the supervision of Konstantinos Dimelis and which will start with the instruction of the Esoteric Philosophy of the Master and Kriya Yoga.

Also, a second branch is already in operation in Kerkyra (Corfu) under the direction of Ioannis Sgouros and Soula Pouliassi, where Esoteric Philosophy, Esoteric Therapeutics and Kriya Yoga are being taught.

The Omakoio of Lamia is expected to extend operations to Kallithea, in Athens.

Finally, the Omakoio of Trikala, apart from its current activities (with 8 years of continual and unhindered operation), is running for the second time in its history, a Complete Course of Instruction – theoretical and practical – of the multifarious work of the Master in Thessaloniki, with the ulterior motive of making His voice heard in the second capital and the potential future foundation of an Omakoio of Thessaloniki.

Some isolated activities are also undertaken by students of the Master in different parts of Greece, such as Komotini, Loutraki of Corinth, Mytilene, etc. where Esoteric Philosophy, Kriya Yoga and certain aspects of Esoteric Therapeutics are presented.

IN THE OMAKOIO OF TRIKALA
THE FOLLOWING DEPARTMENTS
ARE IN OPERATION:

A) PUBLICATION - SALES OF BOOKS
WHOLESALE - RETAIL

All the books written and published by the Metaphysicist, Master Nikolaos A. Margioris (189 books in total) are distributed through the Omakoio of Trikala, Greece. Please ask for the relevant price list. Also, ask for Ilias L. Katsiampas' (Nikolaos A. Margioris' student) book *From the Master's Mouth to the Student's Ear, with a Thorough Glossary of Sanskrit (Philosophic Dictionary, 400 Words) for the Students of Yoga*. The following books by the same author are in press a) *A Comprehensive Analytical Dictionary of Metaphysical Terms* b) *The Systems of Esoteric Therapeutics*.

B) KRIYA YOGA SCHOOL
PSYCHOSOMATIC - THERAPEUTICS

It started operation for the first time in Trikala, in January of 1992. Master of Metaphysics, Yoga and SHIATSU, N. Margioris revived and established the authentic Kriya Yoga. He brought back the genuine Kriya from obscurity and made it known again. He taught it in Greece for the first time in 1981 in the Omakoio of Athens and he wrote his first book without a Master, *Kriya Yoga - A Practical Method of Psychosomatic-Therapy*. In this School, many physical exercises are taught in combination with rhythmical breathing exercises (Pranayama) so that the Nervous and the Muscular system may become stronger, resulting in health and serenity, as well as the release of the trainee from stress and other psychological disturbances. Kriya is the only path which properly prepares the trainee for his initiation to Concentration (Raja Yoga).

C) RAJA YOGA SCHOOL
MIND ELEVATION FROM CONSCIOUSNESS TO HYPERCONSCIOUSNESS

It was established and has been in operation in Trikala since December 5, 1991. Instruction is accompanied by Master Nikolaos Margioris' book *RAJA YOGA*. In Raja Yoga, the advanced students are trained only in intellectual exercises aiming to perfect and balance the Mind. The trainee strengthens his will and acquires a larger and clearer understanding of every matter that may occupy him, particularly in Metaphysics. Special exercises in concentration and hyperconcentration only found in Raja Yoga are executed with the purpose of ultimately and gradually reactivating the third and highest Mind function, hyperconsciousness.

Also all the Yoga systems such as Karma, Bhakti, Mantra, Jnani, Kundalini (Tantra) and so on, are taught.

D) SEMINARS OF SHIATSU - SUGGESTION - HYPNOTISM

Every year, many seminars on Therapeutics without medication based on the Japanese technique of SHIATSU (Namikoshi) are held, while at the same time the ancient Greek method of Massaging (Asclipieia-Amfiaraeia), of Finger-tapping (Nikolaos A. Margioris' method), of Sleep Therapy (suggestion, hypnotism) and others are taught.

E) SEMINARS AND SPEECHES OF ESOTERIC PHILOSOPHY

In these seminars, topics concerning the entire field of Esoteric Philosophy, Occultism and Mysticism, such as the other Dimensions; the Law of Free Will, of Karma and of Reincarnation; the life and work of great Sage Masters; the Body-Mind-Intellect-Soul-Spirit; the Divine Plan and the Evolution of Creation and so on, are presented.

F) ATMOLIQUEFACTION SCHOOL *SLIMMING*

This department of the Omakoio of Trikala operates once or twice a year and its program lasts for about three months. Special physical exercises in combination with the proper breathing exercises (Pranayama - N. Margioris' system) are taught. These are very effective in activating the organism, resulting in perspiration and the burning of fat. At the same time, muscles are strengthened without any mechanical means or medicine.

G) ESOTERIC KEY
STUDIES THROUGH A CORRESPONDENCE COURSE IN THE FOLLOWING BRANCHES OF ESOTERICISM

1) ASTROLOGY - ASTROSOPHY
2) ESOTERIC PHILOSOPHY
3) SCIENTIFIC SPIRITUALISM
4) HYPNOTISM - ORTHOPSYCHISM

5) ESOTERIC THERAPEUTICS
6) ESOTERIC INITIATION
7) MEDITATION
8) DESYMBOLISM

Those who would like further information and analytical prospectuses about any branch may request them from the OMAKOIO OF TRIKALA, 21 Kefallinias Str., 42131, Trikala, Greece, or call **Mr. Ilias Katsiampas** at the telephone number 0030-24310-75505 or 0030-6974-580768 (mobile).

All the books, essays, journals and correspondence courses by Master Nikolaos A. Margioris, founder of the Omakoio of Athens, are available at the Omakoio of Trikala.

BIBLIOGRAPHY OF THE BOOK

The entire Work is the result of the painstaking research, study, processing and composition of multiple elements and details that the director of the Omakoio of Trikala has managed through his sound and certified experience on Esoteric Reality.

His decade-long studies under the immediate close personal tutelage, relationship and cooperation with his Master Nikolaos A. Margioris, the well-found Esoteric Knowledge that he Composed to an incredible degree Within him, his small personal experiences and the uninterrupted contact and cooperation with his fellow students have given him the opportunity to encounter and validate on multiple occasions and levels the Esoteric Knowledge that his Master conveyed to him, especially everything that concerns the Apocalypse of John.

Foremost, however, for the present Work he used certain parts from the Pure Preserved Oral Teachings of his Master that concerned the Explanation of the Apocalypse of John (as it was presented in this book) which has been validated by the widespread Knowledge and Esoteric Theology that he gained from the exhaustive dialogues with the Master as well as from the study of ALL his works independently, especially from the books ***The Birth and Death of the Worlds and the Beings (matter-antimatter-hypermatter, universe-antiuniverse-hyperuniverse), Life After Death*** **and** ***Esoteric Philosophy.***

Below you will find the full Bibliography that the director of the Omakoio of Trikala additionally took into consideration when composing this work.

BIBLIOGRAPHY OF THE WRITER

I) PUBLISHED BOOKS
BY NIKOLAOS A. MARGIORIS
(copyrights belong to his heirs)

1. **Patapios, the Humble Philosopher and Saint from Egypt,** 1st edition in 1970 (156 pages), 2nd edition in 1987 (220 pages), with supplementary and explanatory material, 3rd edition in 2005 (220 pages).

2. **Light in the Dark,** 1st edition in 1975 (300 pages), 2nd edition in 1987 (429 pages) with supplementary and explanatory material, 3rd edition in 2005 (429 pages).

3. **Theurgy Teaches the Eternal Way of the Soul,** 1st edition in 1975 (318 pages), 2nd edition in 1987 (408 pages), with supplementary and explanatory material.

4. **The Other View of Erich Von Daniken's Dogma**, 1st edition in 1976 (318 pages), 2nd edition in 1994 (372 pages), with supplementary and explanatory material. ISBN: 960-7484-00-2.

5. **The Secret of Hatha Yoga**, 1st edition in 1976 (111 pages), 2nd edition in 1977 (155 pages). ISBN: 960-7484-04-5.

6. **Pythagorean Arithmosophy**, 1st edition in 1977 (168 pages), 2nd edition in 1987 (271 pages), 3rd edition in 1993 (276 pages) with supplementary and explanatory material, 4th edition in 2000 (276 pages), 5th edition in 2004 (282 pages). ISBN: 960-7152-06-09.

7. **The Eleusinian Mysteries**, 1st edition in 1978 (99 pages), 2nd edition in 1987 (159 pages), 3rd edition in 1993 (178 pages) with supplementary and explanatory material, 4th edition in 1999 (183 pages). ISBN: 960-7152-11-5.

8. **The Last Day of Socrates**, 1st edition in 1978 (111 pages), 2nd edition in 1988 (152 pages), with supplementary and explanatory material.

9. **The Pharaohs Akhenaten and Tutankhamun**, 1st edition in 1978 (151 pages), 2nd edition in 1991 (311 pages), with supplementary and explanatory material. ISBN: 960-7152-00-X.

10. **The Birth and Death of the Worlds and the Beings** (matter-antimatter-hypermatter, universe-antiuniverse- hyperuniverse), 1st edition in 1979 (195 pages), 2nd edition in 1990 (p 323 pages), with supplementary and explanatory material, 3nd edition in 2009 (323 pages). ISBN: 960-85024-5-4.

11. **Dravidians, the Ancestors of the Greeks (Synopsis) in English**, 1st edition in 1979 (45 pages).

12. **The Reign of Minos, the Great King of Crete**, 1st edition in 1979 (88 pages), 2nd edition in 1997 (105 pages). ISBN: 960-7484-06-1.

13. **Dravidians, the Ancestors of Greeks**, 1st edition in 1979 (88 pages), 2nd edition in 1989 (143 pages), with supplementary and explanatory material, 3rd edition in 1996 (167 pages), 4th edition in 2004 (166 pages).

14. **Eastern and Western White and Black Magic**, 1st edition in 1979 (134 pages),

15. **White Magic**, 2nd edition in 1992 (227 pages) with supplementary and explanatory material. ISBN: 960-7152-03-4.

16. **Barefoot They Dance on Fire (Anastenaria)**, 1st edition in 1980 (95 pages).

17. Post-mortem Life (or Life after Death), 1st edition in 1982 (256 pages), 2nd edition in 1993 (262 pages), 3rd edition in 2010 (262 pages). ISBN: 960-7152-09-3.

18. Raja Yoga, 1st edition in 1983 (208 pages).

19. The Two-Volume Metaphysical Encyclopaedia, 1st edition in 1985/86 (Volume A, 443 pages, Volume B, 752 pages).

20. Kriya Yoga – A Practical Method of Psychosomatic Therapy, 1st edition in 1988 (357 pages), 2nd edition in 2000 (359 pages).

21. The Desymbolism of Greek Mythology, 1st edition in 1988 (521 pages), 2nd edition in 2002 (562 pages).

22. The Three-Dimensional and Four-Dimensional World, 1st edition in 1989 (214 pages), 2nd edition in 2007 (222 pages). ISBN: 960-85024-3-8.

23. Mystical Teachings, Volume A, 1st edition in 1991 (346 pages). ISBN: 960-85024-1-1 SET 960-85024-7-0.

24. Karma. The Law of Retributive Justice, 1st edition in 1989 (373 pages), 2nd edition in 1996 (373 pages), 3rd edition in 2009 (373 pages). ISBN: 960-85024-0-3.

25. **Reincarnation**, 1st edition in 1990 (286 pages), 2nd edition in 2009 (286 pages). ISBN: 960-85024-4-6.

26. **The Chiroplastic Therapeutics of SHIATSU, Volume A**, 1st edition in 1990 (533 pages). ISBN: 960-85024-6-2.

27. **Psychotherapeutics without Medication**, 1st edition in 1991 (325 pages). ISBN: 960-85024-8-9.

28. **Mysticism. Christocentric and Christocratic Mysticism**, 1st edition in 1991 (331 pages). ISBN: 960-85024-9-7.

29. **Occultism (Occultology), Volume A**, 1st edition in 1991 (391 pages). ISBN: 960-7152-01-8, 960-7152-02-6.

30. **Occultism (Occultology), Volume B**, 1st edition in 1992 (428 pages). ISBN: 960-7152-01-8, T.2. 960-7152-04-2.

31. **The Chiroplastic Therapeutics of SHIATSU, Volume B**, 1st edition in 1993 (395 pages). ISBN: SET 960-7152-07-7, 960-7152-08-5.

32. **Mystical Teachings, Volume B**, 1st edition in 1993 (388 pages). ISBN: SET 960-85024-7-0, 960-7152-05-0.

33. **Mystical Teachings, Volume C**, 1st edition in 1994 (379 pages). ISBN: SET 960-85024-7-0, 960-7152-10-7.

34. The Chiroplastic Therapeutics of SHIATSU, Volume C, 1st edition in 1993 (255 pages).

35. Occultism (Occultology), Volume C, 1st edition in 1997, 103 pages. ISBN: 960-7484-05-3.

II) ESSAYS BY NIKOLAOS. A. MARGIORIS

1. SCHOOL OF ASCLEPEANS - HYPNOTHERAPISTS

2. CARL VON REICHENBACH

3. SCHOOL OF ASCLEPEANS – SPIRITUAL THERAPISTS THEOPHRASTUS PARACELSUS

4. MAGNETOTHERAPY

5. ASCLEPIAIA AND AMFIARAEIA

6. THE THERAPY FROM BEFORE TIME

7. THE CELL AND LIFE MYSTERY

8. ECTOPLASM

9. ESSENES

10. APPARITIONS OF IDOLS OF LIVING PEOPLE

11. ANASTENARIA

12. CREATION OF THE WORLDS

13. MYSTICISM

14. DRAVIDIANS, THE FIRST GREEKS OF THE AEGEAN SEA

15. THE CONTROL OF VIBRATIONS

16. WHAT IS ESOTERICISM?

17. THE HOLY SCROLLS OF THE ESSENE RULES

18. EROS AND LOVE

19. PROPER NUTRITION, PROPER DIET, WEIGHT LOSS

20. THERAPEUTICS WITHOUT MEDICATION

21. THERAPEUTICS THROUGH HYPNOTISM

22. THERAPY OF PSYCHOPATHY

23. SHIATSU. THERAPEUTIC METHOD TWO VOLUMES (1st seminar)

24. SHIATSU. THERAPEUTIC METHOD TWO VOLUMES (2nd seminar)

25. SHIATSU. THERAPEUTUC METHOD TWO VOLUMES (3rd seminar)

26. SHIATSU. THERAPEUTIC METHOD TWO VOLUMES (4th seminar)

27. **SHIATSU. THERAPEUTIC METHOD TWO VOLUMES** (5th seminar)

28. **SHIATSU. THERAPEUTIC METHOD ONE VOLUME** (6th seminar)

29. **SHIATSU. THERAPEUTIC METHOD ONE VOLUME** (7th seminar)

30. **SHIATSU. THERAPEUTIC METHOD ONE VOLUME** (8th seminar)

31. **SHIATSU. THERAPEUTIC METHOD ONE VOLUME** (9th seminar)

32. **SHIATSU. THERAPEUTIC METHOD ONE VOLUME** (10th seminar)

33. **SHIATSU. THERAPEUTIC METHOD ONE VOLUME** (11th seminar)

III) OMAKOIO JOURNAL BY NIKOLAOS A. MARGIORIS (49 issues)

The best **metaphysical** *and* **occultist magazine** of our country. **Its every article** *is a* **revelation. Its every page** is an **enlightenment.** It contains **well-documented** *and* **rare metaphysical analyses** on plenty of esoteric matters. It comes in hexads. It was in circulation for **8 years (1977-1985)** in bimonthly publications. The first issue is number 2 and the last is number 49 (total of pages: 1658). There are 8 hexads at **25.00€** per hexad.

IV) ESOTERIC KEY
BY NIKOLAOS A. MARGIORIS

Esotericism and **Metaphysics** are presented in complete form in their practical application and they give the student the **KEY OF KNOWLEDGE**.

Seven Branches *of* **Esotericism**, with **thirty** or **thirty-three** treatises of lessons. Every Branch contains approximately ten or eleven triads or thirty to thirty-three chapters – lessons. See summaries and contents for every branch separately on our site: www.omakoio.gr

Every lesson – triad costs **15.00 Euro. Enrolment** is a one-time fee of **10.00 Euro**. Ask for informative printed enrolment forms for the Esoteric Key branches of study by correspondence course.

The Branches are the following:

1) MEDITATION
2) HYPNOTISM - ORTHOPSYCHISM
3) SCIENTIFIC SPIRITUALISM
4) ESOTERIC PHILOSOPHY

5) ESOTERIC INITIATION
6) ASTROLOGY - ASTROSOPHY
7) ESOTERIC THERAPEUTICS
8) DESYMBOLISM

Nikolaos Margioris' books that are translated into English, or that are currently in the process of being translated, are the following:

1) Dravidians, the Ancestors of the Greeks (translated, in a book), **2) Life after Death** (translated), **3) The Birth and Death of the Worlds and the Beings** (matter, antimatter, hypermatter, universe, antiuniverse, hyperuniverse) (in the process of being translated), **4) Kriya Yoga** (translated) and **5) Raja Yoga** (translated).

BOOKS BY ILIAS L. KATSIAMPAS (N. MARGIORIS' STUDENT) OMAKOIOS OF TRIKALA AND OF THESSALONIKI, GREECE (AND YOGA ACADEMY OF NIKOLAOS MARGIORIS – OMAKOIO)

My own books (**Ilias Katsiampas,** student of **Master N. Margioris**) that relate directly to Margioris' work, translated into English, are the following:

1) 10-year Anniversary of the Establishment of the Omakoio of Athens by Master N. A. Margioris. A bilingual **Greek-English 1999 edition** in an A4 thermal-bound edition, the Greek text consisting of 34 pages and the English text of 33 pages.

2) **A Full and Most Analytical Dictionary – Guide of Metaphysical Meanings**, in press.

3) **Asclepean Art and the Systems of Esoteric Therapeutics**, in press.

4) **Bilingual Greek-English Magazine "New Omakoio"**, size A4, 1st issue, of 100 pages. All the 189 writings of Master Nikolaos Margioris are included in Greek and in English, with a photo of the cover, summaries and contents for each one separately, esoteric articles and the Schools-Omakoios that function in Greece.

5) **Collection of Articles – Advice & Interviews** of Ilias L. Katsiampas, 1st edition in an A4 thermal-bound edition. October 2004. First Reward from the International Union (Company) Greek Man of Letters (DEEL).

6) **Esoteric and Spiritual Experiences of Master Nikolaos A. Margioris.** A bilingual **Greek-English edition** in an A4 thermal-bound edition. 1st edition 2004.

7) **From Deep Metaphysical Correspondence.** In Greek, 1st edition 2007, 400 pages.

8) **From the Master's Mouth to the Student's Ear, with a thorough glossary of Sanskrit (philosophic dictionary, 400 words) for the students of Yoga**, 1st edition 1995 (270 pages), dimensions 24X17,

ISBN: 960-85735-0-5. In the Greek language, it is available in book form. The English translation is also available in an A4 thermal-bound edition.

9) **Handbook – Guide for Staff and Instructors of Esotericism According to Master Nikolaos A. Margioris' Work.** It exists in Greek in an A4 thermal-bound edition (202 pages), 1st edition 2003 and in English as a separate edition (206 pages), **only for the members of the Omakoios.**

10) **Inauguration of the Omakoio of Lamia by Master N. A. Margioris.** A bilingual **Greek-English 2000 edition** in an A4 thermal-bound edition, the Greek text consisting of 36 pages and the English text of 22 pages.

11) **Inauguration of the Omakoio of Trikala by Master N. A. Margioris.** A bilingual **Greek-English 1999 edition** in an A4 thermal-bound edition, the Greek text consisting of 57 pages and the English text of 38 pages.

12) **Meditation and Mysticism, Raja and Kundalini Yoga (Theory and Practice)**, in press.

13) **Plagues and Provocations of our Time. The Metaphysical View.** In press.

14) **Prayer Book and Poems of Master Nikolaos A. Margioris.** A bilingual **Greek-English edition.** In book form. 1st edition 2004. First Reward from the

International Union (Company) Greek Man of Letters (DEEL).

15) **The Apocalypse of John as Explained by Master Nikolaos A. Margioris** (A bilingual Greek-English edition, supervised and with extensive analytical annotations by his student, Ilias L. Katsiampas), 1st edition 1999, ISBN: 960-85735-1-3. Second Award from the International Union (Company) Greek Man of Letters (DEEL).

16) **The Mystery of Death and the Post-Mortem Course of the Soul.** In press.

17) **The Question of Aliens.** In press.

Information
Ilias Katsiampas
21 Kefallinias str., 42131 Trikala, Greece
Tel. and Fax 0030-24310-75505
or mobile: 0030-6974-580768
Website: http://www.omakoio.gr
or https://omakoio.blogspot.com
E-mails: omakoio@omakoio.gr
or omakoeio@gmail.com

GREEK WRITERS WHO USED EXCERPTS
FROM THE 189 WORKS OF THE AUTHOR
AND THE MODERN
METAPHYSICAL MASTER
NIKOLAOS A. MARGIORIS
(AND CITED IT
IN THEIR BIBLIOGRAPHY)
(Search and classification by his student
Ilias L. Katsiampas)

1) *THE DECIPHERING OF THE PHAISTOS DISC - GENESIS THE GREEK SPIRIT DESCENDED FROM SIRIUS* by Thodoros Axiotis, editions Smyrniotakis. It refers to N.A. Margiori's book *Eleusinian Mysteries*.

2) *SEARCHING FOR THE LOST ARK*, by Thodoros Axiotis. Smirniotakis Editions. It refers to the book *Eleusinian Mysteries* by N.A. Margioris.

3) *ARGO - THE FIRST ARGONAUTIC EXPEDITION OF 3.500 B.C.* by Thodoros Axiotis, Smirniotakis Editions. It refers to the book *Eleusinian Mysteries* by N.A. Margioris.

4) *THE CRETAN MYSTERIES*, by George Siettos. Pyrinos Kosmos, Athens 1995 editions. It refers to the book *Light in the Dark*, by N.A. Margioris.

5) *ANCIENT SURVIVALS IN CHRISTIANITY* by Georgios Siettos, Altebaran Editions, Athens 1994. It refers to N.A. Margiori's book *Light in the Dark*, 1975 edition.

6) *THE PYTHAGOREAN MYSTERIES* by Georgios Siettos. Pyrinos Kosmos Editions, Athens 1933. It refers to N.A. Margiori's book *Light in the Dark*, 1975 edition.

7) *PYTHAGORA'S SECRET CODE AND THE DECIPHERING OF HIS TEACHINGS*, by Ippokratis Dakoglou, New Thesis editions, 1st, 2nd, 3rd Volumes. It refers to N.A. Margiori's books *The Two-Volume Metaphysical Encyclopaedia, Theurgy Teaches the Eternal Way of the Soul* and *Pythagorean Arithmosophy*.

8) *EGYPT YESTERDAY AND TODAY,* by Paraskevi Vlahogianni, Protovoulia Editions, Athens 1992. It refers to N.A. Margiori's books *Pythagorean Arithmosophy* and *The Pharaohs*.

9) "PYRAMIS' by Paul Varouchakis. Pyrinos Kosmos Editions, Athens 1992. It refers to N.A. Margiori's books *The Three-Dimensional and Four-Dimensional World, The Birth and Death of the Worlds and the Beings (matter-antimatter-hypermatter, universe-antiuniverse- hyperuniverse), Pythagorean Arithmosophy* and *The Pharaohs* of N. A. Margioris.

10) *THE BASIC PRINCIPLES OF METAPSYCHICS* by Aspasia Papadomichelaki, Center of Metaphysical Information Editions, Athens 1992. It refers to the books *What is Esotericism, Pythagorean Arithmosophy, The Essenes, The Pharaohs, The Eleusinian Mysteries, The Birth and Death of the Worlds and the Beings (matter-antimatter-hypermatter, universe-antiuniverse- hyperuniverse), The Three-Dimensional and Four-Dimensional World, The Control of Vibrations, Esoteric Philosophy* and *Posthumous Life.*

11) *THE MAGICAL WORK*, by Aspasia Papadomichelaki, Athens 1993. It refers to N.A. Margiori's book *Eastern and Western White and Black Magic*, 1st Edition, 1980".

12) *FIREWALKING AND ANASTENARIDES*, by Iassonas Evaghelou, Dodoni Editions. 4th Edition Athens 1994. It refers to N.A. Margiori's book *Walking on Fire - Anastenaria* and to his point of view about Anastenaria.

13) *THE TRUTH ABOUT PREHISTORY, HISTORY AND THE GREEK CIVILIZATION – VOLUME A* by Marinos Razis, Montreal, Quebec, Canada, 1995. It refers to N.A. Margiori's books *The Desymbolism of the Greek Mythology* and *Dravidians, the Ancestors of Greeks*.

14) THE TRUTH ABOUT PREHISTORY, HISTORY AND THE GREEK CIVILIZATION – VOLUME B, by Marinos Razis, Montreal, Quebec, Canada 1997. It refers to the books *The Desymbolism of Greek Mythology, The Two-Volume Metaphysical Encyclopaedia, The Reign of Minos, the Great King of Crete, The Eleusinian Mysteries, Dravidians, the Ancestors of the Greeks,* of N.A. Margioris and to **Ilias Katsiampa's book** *From the Master's Mouth to the Student's Ear.*

15) ON THE PATH OF SELF-KNOWLEDGE (issues about the soul) by Aristidis N. Oihaliotis, Athens 1985. It refers to N.A. Margiori's books *Pythagorean Arithmosophy* and *Dravidians, the First Greeks of the Aegean Sea".*

16) *SAINT PATAPIOS,* by Styl. Papadopoulos, professor at the University of Athens, 1995, The Hermits of the Holy Monastery of Saint Patapios Editions. It refers to N.A. Margiori's book *The Birth and Death of the Worlds and the Beings (matter-antimatter-hypermatter, universe-antiuniverse- hyperuniverse).*

17) *MONISM (Physical Sciences and Philosophy)* by Iasonas Evaghelou, Savvalas Editions, 2nd edition, Athens 1996. It refers to Nikolaos A. Magriori's book *The Birth and Death of the Worlds and the Beings (matter-antimatter-hypermatter, universe-antiuniverse-hyperuniverse)*.

18) *THE PHAISTOS DISC SPEAKS GREEK* by Efi Polighiannaki, Georgiadis Editions, Athens, 1996. It refers to Nikolaos Margiori's English book **Dravidians, the Pre-Hellenic Greeks**.

19) *THE ANCIENT GREEK PANKRATION ATHLETIC EVENT, THE TRUTH ABOUT MARTIAL ARTS - THE FIGHTING ARTS*, by Lazaros E. Savidhis, 1997 edition. It refers to Nikolaos A. Margiori's books **Dravidians, the Ancestors of the Greeks** and *The Reign of Minos, the Great King of Crete*.

20) *THE DELUGE OF DEUCALION*, by Georgios K. Atsalis, 1st edition 1986, 2nd edition 1993, Nea Thesis. It refers to the book *Dravidians, the Ancestors of the Greeks* by Nikolaos A. Margioris.

21) *ASTROBIOCHEMICAL MEDECINE. THE SCIENCE FROM THE PAST, THERAPY OF THE FUTURE*, by Michalis P. Rodopoulos, 1st edition April 1993. It refers to N. Margiori's book *The Three-Dimensional and Four-Dimensional World*.

22) *THE HIDDEN TRUTHS. AN ESOTERIC TREATISE. PLANET EARTH - PART 1*, by Michalis P. Rodopoulos, 1st edition in September 1997. It refers to the illustration of Hydra on the cover of N. Margiori's book under the title *Psychotherapeutics without medicines*, as well as to the internal cover of the book *Posthumous Life*.

23) *PLANET EARTH, ZERO TIME, GREEK SURVIVE, VOLUME C*, by Michalis P. Rodopoulos. It dedicates a whole chapter to Margiori's point of view about the Dravidians, as well as to other references concerning Margiori's esoteric point of view.

24) *ELEUSINIAN MYSTERIES* by Anestis Keramidas, Istoriognosia Editions. There is a reference to the book *Eleusinian Mysteries* by N. A. Margioris.

25) *THE FOREKNOWLEDGE OF THE DELPHI*, by Ioannis Fourakis. It mentions Chattergi's and Margioris' view that the Dravidians are the ancestors of the Greek people who lived in the wider area of the Mediterranean basin.

26) *THE TETRACTYS OF IONIA AND THE IONIAN LANGUAGE*, by Nikolaos Andreadakis, Georgiadi Editions, Athens: 1999.

27) *THE TABOU OF ENLIGHTENMENT* by Eleni Ierodiakonou, Esoptron Editions, Athens: 2008. In Ch. 7 (In Search of a Master) she makes extensive

reference to her meeting and her profoundly positive experience with N.A. Margioris.

28) **THE UNSEEN ASPECT OF THE INDOEUROPEAN ISSUE (THE THEORY OF THE SUBMERGED AEGAEIS)**, by Kostas Skandalis, Georgiadi Editions. It mentions N. A. Margioris' book *Dravidians, the Ancestors of the Greeks*.

29) **VIOLET FLAME, PRACTICAL THERAPEUTICS**, by Nitsele-Eleni Grammatakakis, Andromeda Editions, 2009. The article of N. Margioris about St. Germain or Master Rakoczi, which has been taken from the magazine 'Omakoio' (49 issues in total), is included unabridged in the last chapter of the book (i.e.: the 14th)

30) **PANEGYPTIA** MAGAZINE: A periodic publication of the Egyptiot Greek Association, 25th Year, issue no 147, May-June 2009. N. Nikitaridis' extensive feature article about the character and work of Nikolaos Margioris, as an Egyptiot Greek, and especially about Margioris receiving 60th place among the 100 Greatest Greeks that ever lived. The information for this feature article was taken from the following sources: www.omakoio.gr [18-6-2001] – masonic publications – 'Trito Mati' Magazine, issue 28 [9/1993] and 35 [5/1994].

31) **YOGA, A PHILOSOPHY OF LIFE**, Porfyra Editions, Ed. Sophia Digeni.

It mentions the books *Kriya Yoga* and *Raja Yoga* of Master Nikolaos Margioris, and includes a significant amount of information taken from them, as well as the method of Atmoliquefaction- Weight Loss and Detoxification, which N. Margioris used and taught. His students use it to this day.

32) *IOANNIS A. KAPODISTRIAS, THE SAINT OF POLITICS (THE PAST AND THE PRESENT BASED ON HIS UNPUBLISHED LETTERS)*, by Ioannis S. Kornilakis, Elaia Editions. The book by N. Margioris *Pythagorean Arithmosophy* is mentioned among the books that the author consulted.

33) *HISTORY OF THE FOUNDATION OF THE OSIRIS LODGE No. 117, IN EAST ATHENS. SIXTY YEARS OF BROTHER STAMATI VAZAKOPOULOS' MASONIC JOURNEY. ALSO THE SACRED PARTHENON LODGE, No. 376, EAST ALEXANDRIA,* by Stamatis Vazakopoulos, Athina Editions, 2010.

The book was sent as a complimentary gift to Ilias Katsiampas with the following dedication: 'To the Beloved spiritual child of my co-founder of the Sacred Osiris Lodge, No 117, in East Athens, and first Reverend Brother NIKOLAOS MARGIORIS, and his companion in this spiritual cultivation, ILIAS KATSIAMPAS with immense appreciation and admiration for his Work. The Dean: Stamatis Vazakopoulos, 14/5/2010.'

In this book there are four main references to N. Margioris.

The **first** is on page 11, where there are photos of **Nikolaos Margioris** and **Stamatis Vazakopoulos** with the **caption:** 'The founders of the **Osiris** Lodge, No. 117, in East Athens.'

The **second** reference is by **Stamatis Vazakopoulos** in the *History of the Founding of the Osiris Lodge* No. 117 in East Athens, where, among other things, the following are mentioned:

"*When, after so many years, I visited our first Venerable Brother, the late **Nikolaos Margioris**, one of the first members to conceive and realize the idea that led to the establishment of our Lodge, I relived the ordeal and the unimaginable difficulties that this simple announcement was hiding. It would be a grave omission on my part to not mention that he received the 60th place in the open public vote arranged by the Greek television network SKAI TV in 2008, and was televised in February 2009, in order to discover the '100 Greatest Greeks of ALL time'. This was thanks to the contribution of his massive work to the 'Supernatural Happenings of Our Country'.*

  We emotionally recalled our chance meeting which took place in early September 1962 in Amalia Avenue, where we were surprised to discover that our professional venues were near each other, almost side by side.

...We remembered our being uprooted from Egypt, our adopted country, where we were born, grew up, and had successful careers. But, suddenly, we found ourselves in Greece, strangers among strangers, having left everything behind us: Mothers, Fathers, Wives, children, relatives, friends, homes, careers, our associations, which were bustling with energy, and generally, all the comforts of a cosmopolitan life. We recalled our native Lodges in Egypt...."

*...Also, "Brother **Nikolaos Margioris** conveyed the wish of the Egyptiot Greeks to establish a Lodge in Athens to the former glorious Grand Master Brother Miltiades Pouris, who had been acquainted with him in Egypt. He was convinced of the proposal's seriousness and introduced him to the Grand Master of Greece's Great Lodge, the Reverend Brother Alexandros Tzatzopoulos. Lengthy discussions on Masonic issues followed until the Grand Lodge of Greece was persuaded of the seriousness of our proposal but also our potential for the implementation and success of our goal..."*

The **third reference** includes **three photos** from the first event which was held in **1966** in order to award medals to the founding members of the Osiris Lodge in the presence of the Grand Master of the Grand Orient of Greece, Brother Alexandros Tzatzopoulos. N. Margioris is shown having a conversation with him.

The **fourth reference** comes from a student of the Master in the OMAKOIO Yoga Athens School and our classmate in more recent years, **Alekos Adamidis**, who recently served as Venerable Master of the Osiris Lodge and he notes: *"The history of the establishment and the course of our Sacred Lodge gives to our old, and occasionally new, Brothers the opportunity to remember the personality and virtue of our inspirational Founders and Leaders, and of our late Brother **Nikolaos Margioris**, the First Reverend of our Lodge (between 1964-1965), who left, however, in 1966, in order to establish the School of Philosophy 'OMAKOIO of Athens', and of course the Dean and Brother **Stamatios Vazakopoulos**, who, since 1979, has been the only active founding member from the time when the foundation stone was placed (i.e.: 59 years ago). A loyal fighter serving the ideology of Freemasonry..."*

Finally, relevant details and photographic material for the masonic and other philosophical and didactic activities of Master N. Margioris exist in the work of Ilias Katsiampas, Manager of the OMAKOIO Yoga School in Trikala and Thessaloniki in his book ***Handbook – Guide for Staff and Instructors of Esotericism According to Master Nikolaos -A. Margioris' work***.

34) *ASTROLOGY. THE WORDS OF THE STARS* . Written by Lilian Simou.1st Edition, 2006. Dimeli Editions. The work of N. Margioris *Astrology-Astrosophy* is mentioned in the book's bibliography.

35) **EVAGEIS EN TI KAMINO, (CHARITABLES IN THE FURNACE) A DOCUMENTARY ABOUT THE ANASTENARIA** It was broadcast by ET-3. Production-Direction: Ilias Iosifidis, Zopyros Editions. There is a reference to the book of Nikolaos Margioris *Walking on Fire – Anastenaria*.

36) ***GOD AND MAN. PHILOSOPHICAL VIEWS.*** Olistikis Armonias Editions. It contains the philosophical views of 16 columnists. Two of them mention Nikolaos Margioris and his work.

37) ***COSMOGENESIS: ACCORDING TO THE MEMORY OF NATURE**,* KIVELI EDITIONS. The author Kostas Ollandezos is a student of N. Margioris.

The above mentioned books are just some of the few that have come to the attention of Ilias Katsiampas (Manager of the OMAKOIO Yoga School in Trikala and Thessaloniki and president of the 'YOGA ACADEMY NIKOLAOS MARGIORIS – OMAKOIO') up to this day (December 2010). They draw elements from the work of N. Margioris and make specific references to him and his work in their bibliography.

PRESENTATIONS ON YOUTUBE
AND ON FACEBOOK OF 189 WRITINGS
OF MODERN GREEK MYSTIC
NIKOLAOS A. MARGIORIS (1913-1993)
AND OF 14 BOOKS OF HIS STUDENT
ILIAS KATSIAMPAS
-With English Subtitles-

IN ENGLISH (With English Subtitles)

-VIDEO PRESENTATION IN ENGLISH OF 35 BOOKS OF MODERN GREEK MYSTIC NIKOLAOS A. MARGIORIS (1913-1993).
With English Subtitles. TIME: 61 MINUTES.
http://youtu.be/GUbJ3RbhpIQ
https://www.youtube.com/watch?v=GUbJ3RbhpIQ&feature=youtu.be

-VIDEO OF THE INAUGURATION OF THE NEOPYTHAGOREAN SCHOOL OMAKOIO OF TRIKALA BY GREECE SPIRITUAL MASTER NIKOLAOS A. MARGIORIS THAT TOOK PLACE ON SATURDAY, JANUARY 18th 1992, 20.00 Hrs.
With English Subtitles.
1ST Part of VIDEO (Duration: 2:02:44)
http://youtu.be/KU3JalIc5HI or
https://www.youtube.com/watch?v=KU3JalIc5HI&feature=youtu.be

-VIDEO OF THE INAUGURATION OF THE NEOPYTHAGOREAN SCHOOL OMAKOIO OF TRIKALA BY GREEK SPIRITUAL MASTER NIKOLAOS A. MARGIORIS THAT TOOK PLACE ON SATURDAY, JANUARY 19th 1992, 20.00 Hrs.
With English Subtitles.
2ND Part of VIDEO (Duration: 1:26:15)
http://youtu.be/YR3I-WqVawI or
https://www.youtube.com/watch?v=YR3I-WqVawI&feature=youtu.be

-VIDEO OF THE CELEBRATION OF THE 10 YEARS (1976-1986) SINCE THE FOUNDATION OF THE OMAKOIO OF ATHENS BY MASTER NIKOLAOS A. MARGIORIS, FRIDAY, NOVEMBER 27th, 1987, 21:00.
With English Subtitles.

-AND BANQUET AND SPEECH AT THE GOLDEN AGE HOTEL, ATHENS, WITH AN AWARD OF HONORARY MEDALS BY MASTER NIKOLAOS A. MARGIORIS TO HIS STUDENTS, JULY 1987.
Video Duration: 2h & 7min.
With English Subtitles.
http://youtu.be/D79MIXeDgaE
https://www.youtube.com/watch?v=D79MIXeDgaE&feature=youtu.be
Produced and translated into English by Ilias Katsiampas

SPEECH N. MARGIORIS IN HOUSE OF KROMVAS WITH SUBS IN ENGLISH
Athens 12-3-1988. Video Duration: 1h & 34 min.
https://www.youtube.com/watch?v=luWXYyM36l8

Produced by Ilias Katsiampas and translated into English by Anna Giavasi. Editing: Ilias Katsiampas, Anna Giavasi, Niki Foufa and Mprenta Kathesides and Kimonas Petrocheilos.

PAGES ON FACEBOOK:

NIKOLAOS A. MARGIORIS A GREEK SPIRITUAL MASTER (A MODERN SPIRITUAL FIGURE)
https://www.facebook.com/pages/NIKOLAOS-A-MARGIORIS-A-MODERN-GREEK-SPIRITUAL-FORM/110183632346517?ref=bookmarks

GROUPS ON FACEBOOK
YOGA ACADEMY OF NIKOLAOS MARGIORIS – OMAKOEIO
https://www.facebook.com/groups/848311315181471/

ESOTERICISM FOR ALL - GROUP AND FRIENDS OF NIKOLAOS A. MARGIORIS
https://www.facebook.com/groups/310048335902/

2012-2014 ARRIVAL OR INVASION OF EXTRATERRESTRIAL (ALIENS)?
https://www.facebook.com/

pages/2012-2014-ARRIVAL-OR-INVASION-EXTRA-TERRESTRIAL-ALIENS/223243041058772?fref=ts
PROFILE FACEBOOK ILIAS KATSIAMPAS ADMINISTRATOR OF PAGES-GROUPS
https://www.facebook.com/ilias.katsiampas

SECOND PROFILE FACEBOOK OF ILIAS KATSIAMPAS ADMINISTRATOR OF PAGES-GROUPS
https://www.facebook.com/ekatsiampas?fref=ts

www.ingramcontent.com/pod-product-compliance
Lightning Source LLC
LaVergne TN
LVHW041249080426
835510LV00009B/654